D1380661

8/6

3/m

CONTEMPORARY SCHOOLS
OF PSYCHOLOGY

CONTEMPORARY SCHOOLS OF PSYCHOLOGY

BY

ROBERT S. WOODWORTH
Ph.D., Sc.D.

PROFESSOR OF PSYCHOLOGY COLUMBIA UNIVERSITY

THIRD EDITION

METHUEN & CO. LTD.
36 ESSEX STREET W.C.
LONDON

First Published in Great Britain . . November 5th 1931
Second Edition . . . . December 1937
Third Edition 1943

PRINTED IN GREAT BRITAIN

PREFACE

IN the present age of progressive thinking—no doubt one of the recurring periods of 'illumination' that the world has gone through, and perhaps the greatest of them—a large rôle is being played by the advance of science and by the increasing public acquaintance with science. The new light comes in part from the physical, biological, and medical sciences, but no small measure of it comes from the sciences that deal with human behaviour ; where the darkness has been densest, illumination finds most to reveal. Research on intelligence and motivation, on heredity and environment, are gradually clarifying what have always been matters of conflicting opinion. And besides this slow dawn of psychological knowledge, we are exposed to the blinding flashes of psycho-analysis, behaviourism, and other schools of psychology, some of them little known as yet to the interested public. The light emitted by these radical schools, though still far from steady and serene, does afford revealing glimpses of the unknown.

For anything like a definitive statement of the truth or falsity of the teachings of these several schools, the time is not yet ripe. If one demands only final conclusions, one must wait long decades for the answer. But if one desires to participate in the forward movement of the times and to keep pace with the progress of thought, one will find the schools of to-day well worthy of a hearing.

The present book seeks to provide an objective view of contemporary psychology so far as concerns the schools and their illuminating views of humanity. It does not aim to present the author's own views in any systematic form, though he has not shrunk from personal comments here and there. It does not aim at an exhaustive criticism of the various schools nor at such an evaluation of them as would lead the reader toward one and away from another. Its aim is rather to present an impartial picture of the schools, so that the reader can see the essential features of each one free from confusing detail though with enough concreteness to lend colour to the picture.

The book has grown out of a course of lectures entitled 'A Survey of Contemporary Psychology' which has been repeated several years for audiences of university students and others interested in psychology. The author's thanks are due to many students and colleagues who have offered helpful criticisms at various stages in the long process of producing the book.

R. S. WOODWORTH

COLUMBIA UNIVERSITY
March 25, 1931

CONTENTS

CHAPTER I

CHAPTER II

CHAPTER III

CHAPTER IV

CHAPTER V

CHAPTER VI

CHAPTER VII

CONTEMPORARY SCHOOLS OF PSYCHOLOGY

CHAPTER I

THE BACKGROUND OF OUR CURRENT DISPUTES

IN these chapters I propose to regard all of the twentieth century thus far as being contemporary for our purposes.

These years have been intensely active in psychological circles. The number of psychologists has increased tenfold, and the amount of research has gone up in proportion. Closer contacts have been established with other sciences, both the biological and the social, as well as with practical fields where psychology can be applied—education, medicine, law, business, and industry. But it is not my purpose to survey the gradual accumulation of psychological knowledge, nor to show you the psychologists actually at work in their laboratories and examining rooms. I am not going to set before you the solid results that have been achieved, nor the questions settled to every one's satisfaction. Rather, my object is to bring forward unsettled questions of fundamental importance, questions on which keen debate is going on, doubts whether psychology is on the right track, efforts on the part of one or another leader to steer the group in some new direction.

The past thirty years have been remarkably productive

of new movements in psychology, with the result that we now see the curious phenomenon of schools differing radically from one another in their ideas as to what psychology should be doing and how it should go to work. These schools remind one of schools of philosophy, and are scarcely to be paralleled at present in the other natural sciences. Perhaps their existence in contemporary psychology is a sign of the youth of our science and of the vast number of unexplored possibilities that we have still to examine, as well as of our recent departure from the parental household of philosophy. How important any one of them is can scarcely be told till they have had more time to develop. Meanwhile, they are certainly interesting to any one who wants to obtain suggestive ideas. They are contemporary schools in that all have arisen recently, while none as yet shows any signs of early death.

Before turning our attention to one after another of the new schools, we may well glance briefly at the psychology that preceded our contemporary period. Each school began as a revolt against the established order, and cannot be understood without taking account of its historical background. We should know something of the established order of 1900, against which the present schools have revolted. Now to understand that established order, we have to remember that it was itself at one time new and revolutionary. Any school, no matter how radical it seems at first, is likely to become an established order if it has any success, and in time fresh revolts will arise against it. In fact, we are already witnessing revolts against such modern schools as behaviourism and psycho-analysis on the ground that they are 'traditional.' Similarly, the established order of 1900 was left over from an earlier revolt. Away back at the beginning of the modern scientific movement in the seventeenth century, we find such men as Descartes and Hobbes rebelling against the traditional psychology of that day, and so giving us the beginnings of what we call modern psychology in distinction from the ancient and medieval.

I cannot fairly characterize the pre-modern psychology in a few words, and those who make a careful study of it assure us that there is really much in it that has quite a modern flavour. Valuable insights in psychology have been newly discovered time after time, from the days of Plato and Aristotle to the present. But the pre-modern psychology, as it appeared to the earliest psychologists who can be called modern, suffered from too much complexity, too many irreducible ' faculties,' and too little relationship with the physical world. Sensation, imagination, memory, thought, desire, and bodily motion appeared like so many different types of activity, all of them radically different from the processes of physical nature, which also appeared to be of many distinct types.

THE BOLD BEGINNINGS OF MODERN PSYCHOLOGY

Though we still think of psychology as a young science, we are not to suppose that our generation is the first to attempt lining up mental science with physical. Scarcely had astronomy and physics led off in the early modern scientific movement when the psychologists of the day joined the procession. Early in the seventeenth century, Galileo and others revolutionized physics by showing that many and perhaps all physical processes could be described in terms of motion and inertia ; and Harvey, by discovering the circulation of the blood, made a start toward explaining physiological processes in physical terms. Without delay, Descartes sought to apply physics to the understanding of animal and human behaviour. Behaviour he based on what we now call reflex action ; and a reflex he conceived as a motion of some fluid along the nerves from the sense

organs to the brain and thence back to the muscles.   Thus
the physical force or motion that excited the sense organ
set in motion a physical process within the body that resulted
in muscular movement.   The soul Descartes located in the
brain, and he supposed it to intervene in certain cases
between the incoming and outgoing motions in the nerves.
In animals, however, as he believed, there was no soul, and
all behaviour consisted purely of physical motion.   The
human soul, with its faculty of thinking, he held to be
non-physical.   Hobbes went one better, since for him all
mental as well as bodily processes were reducible to motion.
External motion striking the sense organs was communi-
cated to the nerves, brain, and heart, and the internal
motion, once started, persisted by inertia in the form of
memories and ideas.   He reduced all mental processes to
the common basis of motion and thus brought them into
line with physical processes.   Hobbes's revolt against the
faculty psychology was certainly radical, but it was sketchy
in detail ;   so that the task remained for the English psychology of the succeeding century to develop this line of
thought, as it did in the ' association psychology.'

The associationists, the progressive psychologists of the
eighteenth and early nineteenth centuries, tried to reduce
all mental processes to the single process of association.
They gave up Hobbes's inadequate notion of memories as
persisting by mere inertia, and sought to explain them by
the linkage of one process or ' idea ' with another.   When
two processes had been linked in a person's experience, and
one of them was later thrown into activity by some external
cause, it would in turn arouse the other by virtue of this
linkage or association.   The associationists found it easy
to show how the sequence of thoughts in reverie could be
brought about by previously formed associations between
the thoughts that successively emerge.   They further
showed how the sight of an object, associated in experi-

ence with the feel of it, came to serve as a sign of the presence of the object, and they showed how by similar signs the size and distance of objects could be recognized. They explained that many fears and antipathies could originate in childhood from the association of perfectly innocuous objects or persons with other things that naturally arouse fear or dislike. In similar ways they reduced reasoning, inventing, belief, and action to the one process of association. They studied the laws of association, aiming to reduce them to a single law, and they noted that associations differed in strength according to the frequency, recency, and vividness of the experiences in which they were formed and renewed. With many variations in their views regarding the physical nature of associations, with many applications of their theory to morals, economics, and the social sciences in general, and in spite of numerous objections raised by their contemporaries to their whole doctrine or to parts of it, the associationists grew in influence and dominated the established order in the psychology of the early nineteenth century.

The New Psychology of the Nineteenth Century

But just as the physics of Galileo's time had an immediate influence on psychology, so, early in the nineteenth century, two newly developed sciences made themselves felt. The wonderful achievements of chemistry led to the idea of a ' mental chemistry ' which should analyse mental compounds into their elements. Some of the associationists used this idea to explain why many sensations, such as the colour brown, the feel of hard or soft, moist or dry, the tone of a violin, and the so-called taste of an orange, which is largely smell, could seem simple and unitary though demonstrably due to complex stimuli—just as the compound water seems as simple and unique as its chemical elements, oxygen and hydrogen. The term association was stretched to cover all sorts of combinations, though, as must be admitted, it lost much of its explanatory value in being thus stretched. However this may be, the notion of an analytical psychology that should take its cue from chemistry and work out elements and compounds in the mental sphere, took firm hold at that time.

The influence of physiology was more far-reaching than that of chemistry, for the reason that psychology is closer to physiology in its problems and in its possible methods. Early in the nineteenth century, when physiology began to make effective use of experiment, it blazed a trail for the advance of its sister science. Out of the physiological laboratory grew the psychological laboratory, though it was not till 1879 that Wundt at Leipzig founded the first active psychological laboratory. Soon there were many laboratories, and the ' new psychology,' as it was in 1900, was experimental psychology. It had revolted from the earlier psychology in respect to method and scientific standards, rather than in respect to theory. Where the earlier psychologist had been content to draw his evidence from memory and common experience, with all their uncertainties, this new psychology insisted that data must consist of definite recorded observations. Experiments on the senses and muscular movement had been supplemented by cleverly designed experiments on memory and learning, and hope was strong that all psychological questions could in time be attacked by the new method.

We have not yet displayed the full scope of the psychology of 1900, and our sketch of the nineteenth century would be very incomplete if we omitted to mention the influence of two further sciences that developed rapidly during that period. General biology, and especially the theory of evolution, from 1860 on, brought into view a whole mass of problems that were foreign to the older psychology and also to physiology, chemistry, and physics. Evolution raised the problems of development and of variation. Mental development in the individual and in the race as influenced by heredity and environment, child psychology, animal psychology, differences between individuals and between races, and similar topics began to appear in psychological writings toward the end of the nineteenth century, largely through the influence of Darwin and Galton. Psychology thus came into close contact with zoology and anthropology. Tests for measuring individuals were first devised for use in such studies and were added to the laboratory type of experiments as part of the psychologist's stock of methods.

The remaining influence that calls for notice came from psychiatry ; and the history of psychiatry in the nineteenth century would well repay extended study. Suffice it to say that the treatment of the insane, the neurotic, and the feeble-minded advanced during the century from an utterly unscientific to a highly promising state. Beginning with a classification of the types of abnormal behaviour, scientific psychiatry advanced to a study of the life-history of abnormal people. All through the century, psychiatrists were divided into psychic and somatic camps, the one seeking causes in the mental sphere and the other positing some brain lesion or disturbance behind every abnormality of behaviour. Brain disturbance was actually found in some abnormal conditions, but could not be demonstrated in others. Where it could not be demonstrated with the methods at hand, the somatists assumed it to exist in some elusive form ; and on the whole the somatists were the dominant party among the psychiatrists, and had the most influence on the psychology of the time.

These outside influences that made themselves felt in the psychology of the nineteenth century, raising new problems and leading to the development of new methods of investigation, tended to divorce psychology from its old union with philosophy and to aline it with the natural sciences. But the divorce did not take place all at once. We must remember that psychology had been written by philosophers for two thousand years, and that it was taught by philosophers all through the nineteenth century. When I first made the acquaintance of psychology, about 1890, it was quite bound up with philosophy. It was taught by a philosopher as an integral part of the course in philosophy. The greatest psychologists of that day, such as Wundt and William James, were also philosophers. James, after writing his great *Principles of Psychology*, turned his attention mostly to philosophy and is best known to-day as the forceful and winning exponent of pragmatism. Even in his *Psychology* you will find many discussions which to-day would be regarded as belonging to philosophy rather than to psychology. The philosophers, one may say, had the upper hand at that time, and treated psychology as a subordinate part of their subject. But the experimental or ' new ' psychologists were not meekly accepting the situation. They were urging the claims of psychology to independence. Beginning about 1890, they succeeded in having professorships and departments of psychology established in the universities. They were founding journals and psychological societies. They did not need in the least to disparage philosophy, but simply to urge that psychology, though still a young science, had grown up sufficiently to leave the parental roof, following the example of the older sciences. It needed its independence in order to develop its own technique, to make its own contacts, to formulate its own conceptions, and to attack problems which, while perhaps trivial or meaningless to the philosopher, emerged from the study of man and promised to lead to a better understanding of man's curious ways.

We have been speaking of the work of the psychologists of the later nineteenth century rather than of their theories and formulas. When they tried to give a formal definition of their subject, and to mark off its domain, they were apt to reach some such statement as that psychology was the science of consciousness. James begins by stating that, ' Psychology is the Science of Mental Life, both of its phenomena and of their conditions. The phenomena are such things as we call feelings, desires, cognitions, reasonings, decisions, and the like.' [1] Wundt, in 1892, said that, ' Psychology has to investigate that which we call internal experience—i.e. our own sensation and feeling, our thought and volition—in contradistinction to the objects of external experience, which form the subject-matter of natural science.' [2] Sometimes consciousness was regarded as an inner world, distinct from the world of nature outside. Sometimes, in view of the evident fact that the data of any science are obtained by observers and are in the first instance their conscious experiences, psychology was said to deal with the same sort of data as any other science, but to utilize the data in its own way for the study of consciousness itself and not for the study of the objects of which the observer is conscious. But, in either way of looking at the matter, psychology was limited by definition to the study of consciousness, and to the individual as an experiencer. In conformity with the definition, the primary method of psychological observation was said to be introspection, the report by an individual of his own conscious experiences. The experimental laboratory, said Wundt, was not designed in the least to do away with

[1] W. James, *Principles of Psychology* (Macmillan, 1890), vol. i. p. 1.

[2] W. Wundt, *Lectures on Human and Animal Psychology*, translated by J. E. Creighton and E. B. Titchener (Allen & Unwin, 1894), p. 1.

introspection, but rather to afford the best facilities for accurate and minute introspection.

In the laboratory, however, psychology declined to be limited by the formal definition. The subject in an experiment was not always treated as an experiencer, but often as a performer. The question up for investigation might be how quickly he could react, or how accurately he could perceive, or how completely he could recall material which he had memorized ; and he was not asked to report his experience during the performance, but simply to perform his task. How well he performed it was observed by the experimenter. Again, in studying the feelings and emotions, a common practice was to harness the subject into recording apparatus which would give a tracing of his breathing or pulse. In theory, these objective methods were justified in the psychological laboratory simply as throwing some light, indirectly, upon feelings and other conscious experiences ; but as the researches worked out, the real interest was found to lie in the performance itself. If the subject did report any incidental introspections, they were used to throw light upon his performance, rather than the other way around. Psychology was finding its job and how to do it by the process of exploring its field, rather than from the dictates of theory and formal definition.

We have, then, a picture of the psychologists of about 1890–1900 as an active and aggressive group, small in number but rapidly recruiting itself from the younger generation, hopeful of its newly developed technique of experiments and tests, finding new fields to explore year by year, beginning to study the child, the animal, and the abnormal person as well as the standard adult, maintaining contact on different sides with the workers in other sciences, and much disposed to break loose from philosophy and set up an establishment of its own. In theory, the psychologists of 1900 subscribed to the definition of psychology as the science of consciousness, but in practice they were studying performance as well as experience. In theory they were for an analytical psychology patterned after chemistry, with elementary sensations, images, and feelings, and with complex thoughts and emotions composed of these elements in varying combinations ; but in practice they often disregarded this scheme. In theory they were mostly associationists, but not dogmatically so ; the high noon of associationism was already past. In theory they were strong for a physiological psychology, but in practice they made a profound bow to the brain and passed on their way, since cerebral processes were still too obscure to afford much insight into mental processes.

THE NEW PSYCHOLOGIES OF THE TWENTIETH CENTURY

Such was the established order of 1900 from which the contemporary schools have revolted. We might wonder what there was about it to prompt so many vigorous revolts. It was not so well established nor so orderly as to bore or hamper the enterprising young psychologists of the time. It was incomplete at many points, to be sure, and it did not fully measure up to the demands of scientific method ; moreover, its theory and its practice were rather out of step. But, as psychologists ourselves, we must recognize that the question was not whether the old order was endurable, but whether there was anything in it open to attack. Every young man coming into the game and desiring to make a name for himself looks around for something to attack. If he goes calmly ahead accepting things as they are nobody will pay attention to him. He looks for flaws, and the bigger they are the better he likes them. Enterprising young psychologists at the turn of the century proceeded to pick flaws, and among them the poor old nineteenth-century psychology was pretty well picked to pieces. Schools were started which disagreed with each other fully as much as with the older psychology, and the result has been a very lively period with order not yet re-established.

You are all acquainted with some of the schools that have emerged. Behaviourism, for instance, is known to every one as some sort of a radical movement in psychology. If I asked each of you to tell exactly what behaviourism means, and in what way it revolted from the established order of 1900, I might get many different answers. In fact, it is a fascinating rather than an easy task to discover the real nature of behaviourism. Probably you would all say, and correctly, that the behaviourists objected strenuously to psychology as the science of consciousness, and to introspection as a method for use in the study of man.

But there were other psychologists, and especially psychiatrists, very different from the behaviourists in their background and way of thinking, who agreed with them to this extent, that they decidedly did not regard the study of consciousness as the be-all and end-all of psychology. Those who had to do with abnormal mentality and with maladjusted individuals were inclined even before 1900, and much more since then, to insist that the biggest field for psychology was precisely the unconscious. Here we glimpse the origin of that other modern school of which every one knows—the school of psycho-analysis. Every one probably has some impression of psycho-analysis, and would say that it concerned itself with unconscious ' complexes ' and with the psychology of sex, but beyond that our several impressions might not wholly agree.

While the names of behaviourism and of psycho-analysis have become public property, and while both schools claim to be the ' new psychology ' of the present day, there are other less known schools which are regarded by the psychological fraternity as of similar importance. One of these is the purposivist school, which is not entirely dissimilar from psycho-analysis, though it arose in the effort to create a significant social psychology rather than in the effort to cure the maladjusted individual. You see from its name that this school stresses the fundamental importance of purpose, striving, and goal-seeking. It revolted against the intellectualistic one-sidedness of the nineteenth century. It raised the question, and still keeps the question alive, whether either introspection or the ultra-simple methods and ideas of the behaviourists are ever going to lead to an understanding of human behaviour.

The three schools thus far mentioned all rejected the notion that psychology was essentially the science of consciousness, though they rejected this notion in different ways. Psycho-analysis exalted the unconscious, purposivism held that consciousness was only a part of the field of psychology, and the behaviourists sought to banish consciousness altogether from psychology. But we must not suppose that the 'consciousness' psychologists took all this punishment lying down. They had plenty of fight in them, and reacted by seeking to tune up their introspective method and to clarify their own conceptions of what they were about. As a result, we find emerging among the introspectionists a new school—partly new, at least—which goes by the name of existentialism. Besides its insistence upon refined and precise introspection, this school urges that neither the older psychology nor the modern schools are sufficiently existential or matter-of-fact to guide psychology toward the goal of an advanced science such as physics or chemistry. The psycho-analysts, the purposivists, and the behaviourists are all concerned to make psychology practical in one way or another. They seek to make it more human, and certainly one would suppose that psychology ought to be human. But is that the line of scientific progress? How did physics and chemistry reach their high level of development, and how did the engineering arts based on these sciences gain their extraordinary control over the forces of nature? Not by sticking close to human needs, but by following up phenomena which at first seemed to have no human interest at all. If you open a book on physics, you do not expect to find a chapter on the wheelbarrow, and another on pumps, nor even one on the radio, though these useful human objects may be brought in as illustrations of fundamental principles. Possibly, if psychology could forget its pumps and wheelbarrows, and concentrate its attention upon its elementary matters of fact, it would in time escape from the obvious and discover fundamentals as surprising and revolutionary as electricity or the X-rays. Such is the hope of existentialism.

I have mentioned four of the contemporary schools which will come before us for closer study, and the remaining one has recently been somewhat in the public eye, though its name is perhaps more baffling than enlightening. This is the school of Gestalt psychology, a school of German origin, sometimes called configurationism for want of a better English name. I am afraid I cannot give you any clear first impression of this school, though it is a school of undeniable importance and may hold the key to the future. I can say just this about it, that its revolt was against the mental chemistry ideal of nineteenth-century psychology. The Gestalt psychologists tell us that any such ideal is a will-o'-the-wisp. Analysis of either experiences or performances into their elements is never going to get us far, they believe. We must take an act or experience as a whole and study it in its setting, rather than attempt to analyse it. Introspectionists and behaviourists alike, according to the Gestalt point of view, are still hopelessly floundering in the barren associationism of past centuries,

With all these divergent movements going on, contemporary psychology might be expected to show no coherence at all, but curiously enough the psychologists of the day still enjoy meeting and discussing the problems of psychology, and still treat one another with respect. The science has not broken apart but has become, if anything, more unified. We shall wish to give some attention to this unity amid all the diversity of the schools. The mutual respect of psychologists reflects the obvious zeal shown by members of all schools for the continued progress of the science. Some schools are more concerned to make psychology scientific and others to make it more human and adequate. One would like to see it both scientific and adequate, and the psychologists keep together in the hope that such results can be achieved.

Another reason for the continued unity of psychology is found in the fact that only a minority of psychologists have become active adherents of any of the schools. Some may lean toward one school and some more toward another, but on the whole the psychologists of the world are proceeding on their way in the middle of the road. After all, there was much in the psychology of 1900 against which there has been no revolt. Many of the results of previous research still hold good, and fresh research during the past thirty years has added many new results that have no connexion with any of the schools. The psychologists of 1900 were on their way, and their way is our way, only that we seem to be further ahead. Yet I would not say that the schools are merely decorative touches on our contemporary psychology, nor that they have been ordained simply for our entertainment during these busy years. They are serving to enlarge our view and to clarify it. Each shows elements of vitality and is probably here to stay. It is a good thing that there are several of them. Probably no one of them has the full vision of what psychology is destined to achieve. One shows us one alluring prospect, another another. Without aspiring in this year of grace to synthesize them all into a complete conception of what psychology ought to be and do, we may hope to catch the positive contribution that each is prepared to make to our understanding. In this hope we shall afford each one an opportunity to tell its story, before finally giving a brief glimpse at the large body of psychologists who are steadily advancing in the middle of the road.

CHAPTER II

INTROSPECTIVE PSYCHOLOGY AND THE EXISTENTIAL SCHOOL

INTROSPECTION as a psychological method of observation is not the property of any school, nor is the objective method the property of any school, as is shown by the fact that many psychologists have employed both methods and have often done so in the same investigation. Behaviourists have denied the value of introspection, but there are no introspectionists who have denied the value of objective methods in behaviour study nor the value of behaviour study as a side line to psychology. Consequently, we cannot speak of the introspective school as if all psychologists who employed introspection in their work formed a compact body, united by their loyalty to this method of study. Nor can we properly speak of the nineteenth-century psychology as exclusively introspective and of objective methods as emerging in our own times ; for objective methods have been used since the beginning of experimental psychology, in the study of reaction times and accuracy of perception and later in experiments on memory and learning. What we do find at the end of the last and the beginning of the present century is an expansion of the field in which introspection was seriously attempted, with constructive criticism of the method and more precise formulation of the aim of introspective psychology. The ' Existential Psychology ' which thus emerged I connect particularly

2

with the vigorous teachings of the late Professor Edward Bradford Titchener.

I suppose we should all agree, whatever be our leanings toward any school, that psychology's task is to study the individual. Its data consist of observations of the individual's doings. If the individual is a human being capable of making a report, we may ask him to observe and report something of his own doings, or of what is happening to or in him. If we call the individual studied the 'subject,' we may call the observations which he thus reports subjective observations, using the correlative term, objective, for observations made upon him by another person. Introspection is subjective observation. Sometimes all observations contributed by the subject are called introspective, and sometimes this term is limited to certain more complex, or more refined, types of subjective observation, as I shall explain later.

If we bear in mind that introspection has been under fire of late, the behaviourists insisting that only objective methods of observation have any claim to scientific validity, we shall find a twofold interest in rapidly reviewing samples of psychological work carried out by aid of subjective observation. We shall see what it is, in the concrete, that the behaviourists wish to eliminate from psychology, and we shall be leading up to the existential school.

SAMPLES OF INTROSPECTIVE PSYCHOLOGY

Strange as it may seem, psychology learned the use of the subjective method of observation not from philosophy but from physics and physiology. Physics used it in studying light and sound, and physiology in studying the sense organs. Light and sound, we must remember, are not absolutely objective facts, for light is not simply radiation, but visible radiation, and sound is not simply vibration, but audible vibration. There is much vibration that is not audible and much radiation that is not visible. Mix pure red light and pure yellow light and objectively you have nothing but just that mixture, but the observer into whose eyes you throw this mixture sees an orange colour. Mixture of sounds gives entirely different results, because the ear is a different sort of registering instrument from the eye. The physicists had been interested in these subjective phenomena from the time of Newton down. With the rapid development of physiology early in the nineteenth century, some of the physiologists began to experiment on the function of the sense organs. How should they examine the operation of these organs ? The obvious way was to apply a stimulus to a sense organ and ask the individual to report what impression it made, what sensation he got. This form of the subjective method of getting data may be called the method of impression. It is subjective because the subject on whom or in whom the impression is made observes and reports it. The physiologist usually experimented on himself first. He applied a certain stimulus to one of his own sense organs and noted the impression received. To verify his own observations he had other persons serve as subjects in the same experiment, and if every one reported the same impression from the same stimulus, he accepted the fact as an established fact bearing on the operation of that sense organ. Great quantities of accepted results were obtained by this method of impression all through the nineteenth century by physicists and physiologists and latterly by psychologists.

One general problem in the study of the senses is that of analysis, the search for the elementary sensations. For example, the skin sense gives us any number of impressions : the shape, size, weight, and texture of objects, warmth, cold, moisture, and dryness, roughness and hardness—an

indefinite number of facts.   But the probability was that
the sense did not exactly *give* us all these facts, but gave
certain elementary data which served as indicators of the
facts.   The problem was to discover the elementary data,
and in the course of time it was found that there were
certainly four elementary sensations from the skin—
warmth, cold, pain, and pressure—and that probably all
the other impressions were blends of these four.   This
analysis was achieved by exploring the skin with different
stimuli and finding little spots sensitive to warmth, other
spots sensitive to cold, and so on.

In somewhat the same way, the sense of taste was
analysed.   To our ordinary way of thinking, there are an
indefinite number of varied tastes.   We know, indeed,
that a cold in the nose reduces this variety considerably,
and experimentally it is shown that if the nose is kept out
of the game the number of real tastes goes down to four :
sweet, sour, bitter, and salty.   The numerous tastes that
we ordinarily think of are blends of these with odour, touch,
and temperature sensations.   In the case of lemonade,
we are helped in analysing the blend by knowing how the
stimulus is compounded.   We know that the stimulus
contains sweet and sour and cold, and we know that a
lemon is more than just sour, and that vinegar or sulphuric
acid could not be satisfactorily substituted for it.   It has a
peculiar odour as well.   So lemonade combines the stimuli
for four elementary sensations, and the taste of lemonade
is a blend of the four.   By calling it a blend we mean that,
in spite of its composition, it seems to be a unitary
impression.

The sense of sight furnishes certainly an indefinite
number of impressions, and has the property of spreading
them out in space and giving form and location.   Analysis
indicates six elementary sensations, white, black, red,
yellow, green, and blue, with an enormous variety of blends.

The sense of hearing is different in having no small number of elements, for apparently each tone, high, low, or medium, is as elementary as every other. There are thousands of elements here. But there are blends also in great number, and the analysis of tonal blends has been one of the most striking achievements of this whole line of study. The different characteristic qualities of different instruments are found to depend on different combinations of over-tones with the fundamental tone that is being sounded at any time. In much the same way, the different vowels and consonants are blends of accessory mouth tones with the fundamental tone emitted by the vocal cords. Of late years, telephone and radio engineers have laboured intensively in this field of auditory sensation, as the illuminating engineers have in the field of vision. Their methods have been, first, to control the stimulus by aid of their knowledge of physics, second, to obtain the services of reliable observers and to make conditions as favourable as possible for easy and accurate observation, and then to apply their controlled stimuli and have their reliable observers report the impressions received. They have to depend on the method of impression, because they are not concerned simply with the physics of light or sound, but with the effects produced upon the human being who sees or hears.

The sense of smell long resisted analysis, but recently some progress has been made. Henning [1] gathered a great variety of odorous substances, and presented them to his subjects with careful instructions to this effect : ‘ Forget all you know about the sources of different odours, and simply compare these odours, noting their similarities, till you can arrange them into some order or system.’ Such instructions were needed because the subjects were disposed, otherwise, to try to identify the odours, which

[1] H. Henning, *Der Geruch*, 1924.

effort threw them back upon what they already knew, upon their everyday rough-and-ready classification of odours, and did not make for progress. But when the observers were pinned down to resemblances and differences between the presented odours themselves, with no extraneous considerations admitted, they found certain outstanding odours, much like elements, and other odours which appeared as blends. The experiment illustrates a refinement of subjective observation in the direction of genuine description of one's experience ; one attempts to say what is actually there rather than to say what it happens to suggest. One endeavours to stay within the phenomena to be reported, and describe them by comparison one with another.

Just one more example of the use of the method of impression in the study of the senses. If you look steadily at a coloured spot for twenty or thirty seconds, and then turn the eyes upon a plain grey background, you see a spot of colour complementary to that of the original spot— purple for green, blue for yellow, etc. This 'negative after-image' is a subjective sensation, because there is no objective spot on the plain background. The after-image reveals the complex way in which the eye and brain respond to light, and is an extremely important fact in the physiology and psychology of colour vision. It is even important practically, since one has to make allowances for after-image effects in matching and comparing colours. After-images can easily be demonstrated to any one by trying the experiment on him. But from the nature of the case you can never see any one's after-image but your own. The evidence for this universally accepted fact, then, rests entirely on the method of impression, that is, on subjective observation. In the face of this situation, how any one can deny all validity to subjective observation is a puzzle.

Subjective Observation not Radically Different from Objective

We have been calling the method of impression a form of subjective observation, since the subject makes the report of the impression received by himself. But the question remains whether this subjective observation is really anything different from our ordinary observation of external facts. The method of impression is given prominence by the introspective psychologists, who regard it as the typical case of simple psychological observation, and it is disliked by the behaviourists as tainted with subjectivism. But to the subject himself, who makes the observation, it seems as objective as the observation of an objective fact. You throw a light into his eyes, and he reports, ' It is green.' You put a substance in his mouth, and he reports, ' It is bitter.' You sound a faint tone, and he says, ' Now I hear it—now I don't.' It seems to him the same sort of observation that he is constantly making on objects, except perhaps that he is more painstaking in the experiment. Even in the case of the after-image, he is apt to say, ' I see a purple spot on the wall ; it moves when I move my eyes ; now it is fading out.' He may convince himself that the after-image is something ' in his eyes ' rather than actually on the wall, but the observation seems as objective as any other. There is just one difference : in observing the after-image he leaves aside the question whether there is any real purple spot out there, and simply reports what his eyes tell him, whereas in ordinary life he is concerned with what is really out there and learns to discount and disregard the after-images which his eyes are constantly presenting him. The method of impression requires the observer to lay aside his usual preoccupation with the practical significance of his impressions so that he can report the impressions themselves. But a similar requirement is made in all painstaking observation. Ordinarily, in rough or easy observation, we get a complex impression that serves as a ready sign of some objective fact, and we do not need to notice the impression carefully, because the objective fact is so obviously indicated. But when the impression is faint or obscure, and when it is important to be sure of the objective fact, we are driven to notice the impression itself, so as to make sure of what we actually see or hear. We ask, ' Is there a faint speck out there on the water, or do my eyes deceive me ? ' ' Do I hear a low droning sound, or am I imagining it ? ' We hold interpretation in check till we can make sure of our indicators.

If the method of impression is fundamentally unsound, then, it would seem, all scientific observation is unsound, since it makes practically the same demands on the observer. Let us suppose that a chemist has a great many specimens of water to be examined in order to determine which of them contain any iron, and that he adds to each specimen a certain reagent which produces a blue tinge in the water that contains iron ; and suppose he says to himself, ' If I had an assistant with a good pair of eyes whom I could trust to observe accurately, I could save myself much routine work.' He advertises, and a young girl applies for the job. He fixes up some test tubes with solutions of iron and others with no iron, notes down which are which, and then puts them before the girl, explaining that the job is to examine each test tube carefully so as to be sure whether or not it shows any tinge of blue. Suppose he finds her very accurate and employs her. He then proceeds to place his unknown specimens in her hands and to depend upon her to report which show the blue and which not. First he tested the girl ; now he is testing his specimens. But the girl's job is the same throughout. She is reporting impressions throughout, but her attitude is objective throughout. The chemist used the same procedure first to make a psychological test of his observer and then to make a chemical test of his specimens of water. The observations were the same, but they were used first for a psychological purpose and later for a chemical purpose. At first the chemist used known specimens to find out something about an unknown person ; later he used the now known person as observer to discover something about unknown specimens.

The human observer may be likened to a sensitive recording instrument, such as a thermometer. When you are testing a new thermometer, you apply known temperatures to it and note whether it registers the temperatures correctly. When you have found it accurate, you apply unknown temperatures to it and accept its readings as true of the objective fact. In a psychological experiment, the investigator arranges to know the stimulus that he applies to his subject, and so is able to utilize the subject's response as indicating something about the subject himself and the processes that go on in him. In a chemical or physical experiment, the investigator knows and trusts his observer, and uses his response as an indicator of some otherwise unknown objective fact. Thus the method of impression and the typical scientific observation do not differ as observations but only in what precedes and follows them. They are the same to the observer, but different to the investigator because he starts from a different place and goes in a different direction.

The checks on the method of impression are the same as the checks upon scientific observation in general. They are the agreement of different observers and the consistency of the facts reported. To be sure, individuals differ so much that we cannot expect universal agreement of observers in a psychological experiment. An appreciable percentage of people will match a bluish green, a reddish purple, and a dead grey of the right brightness, and report that they are all exactly the same. Such an individual, we say, has a peculiar colour sense. We test him in various ways, and decide that he is colour-blind, red-green blind. In chemical work, we should rule him out as unsuited to make colour observations. But in psychology, we are pleased to find him, because his peculiarities throw light upon the processes of colour vision. It is just as if a chemist should find one of his instruments recording inaccurately, and, instead of simply throwing it away, should study it with a view to learning something of the inner workings of instruments. The psychologist is by profession a student of a certain type of instruments.

Something was said in the last chapter about experience and performance as the subject-matter of psychology. The method of impression can be regarded from either angle. The elementary sensations, warmth, blue, bitter, and the rest, are facts of experience, and mental chemistry regards them as the elements of which experience is composed. Blends and after-images, also, are facts of experience. But in receiving and reporting impressions, the subject is a performer as well as an experiencer ; and since the experimenter knows the stimulus which he has applied and also knows, or may know, the typical response to be made to that stimulus, he can add to the subject's observation an observation of his own, namely, how well the subject's response corresponded to the stimulus. This observation of correctness or error, made by the experimenter, comes under the head of objective observation. It is an objective fact that the colour-blind individual matches grey, bluish green, and reddish purple. If you ask him why he does so, he says it is because they look alike to him. The behaviourist, or ultra-objectivist, doesn't care how they look to the subject, but only what the subject says or does with regard to them. If our chemist who tested the young girl were a behaviourist, he might say, ' I don't care whether she *sees* blue or not, provided she says blue at the right times and not otherwise. I don't admit,' he might continue, ' that there is any such thing as seeing, apart from verbal or other motor response, any more than I admit that my thermometer feels the temperature which it registers. All I admit, in either case, is a motor response which corresponds to the stimulus.' Well and good—but sometimes the chemist examines his test tubes himself, and reports ' blue ' or ' not blue ' ; and he probably would admit that he said so because he saw them so. For him to deny that the other observer's reports are like his own in this respect, or, in general, for the behaviourists to deny that the method of impression furnishes reports of actual experience, seems fanatical to say the least. Perhaps they don't mean to go so far, and yet you will find them religiously avoiding the use of words like ' see ' and ' hear,' and speaking instead of ' response to light or to sound.'

FURTHER DEVELOPMENT OF THE INTROSPECTIVE METHOD

We might now show how the method of impression was adapted to the study of feelings and aesthetic preferences, the subject being asked whether the presented object was pleasing, or which of two objects was the more pleasing, and we might speak of several other uses of this general method. But it will be more to our purpose to pass on to the development of the method of impression into something more complex which can properly be called introspection.

When you receive a stimulus, your total experience is richer than the mere direct impression you receive from the stimulus. The method of impression calls on you simply to report the direct impression, while the expanded method of introspection calls on you to report your entire experience of the moment, or as much of it as you can. In a laboratory experiment, the subject is concentrated upon his task, so that extraneous thoughts may not be there to be reported. But no matter how concentrated he is upon the stimulus presented, his experience is more than a bare impression of that stimulus, and it is quite possible that a full picture of his momentary experience would throw light on the process he goes through in observing the stimulus.

Suppose that two stimuli are presented for the subject to compare. Would not a full report of his experience probably throw some light on the way the subject achieves his task, i.e. on the process of comparison ? In the classical experiment in weight lifting, the subject lifts first one weight and then another differing but slightly from the first, and judges which is the heavier. How can he do this ? The sensation received from the first weight disappears when he sets that weight down, and yet somehow he compares the second weight with it. The older psychologists had a ready answer in terms of images. The subject, they said, retained an image of the feel of the first weight after setting it down, and could place that image alongside of the sensation received from the second weight. But why not get him to describe his experience and see whether this neat logical scheme is borne out ? The experiment was tried, and the logical scheme was not borne out. The subject would often report that he did not and could not recall how the first weight felt after he had set it down ; he seemed practically to forget the first weight, and simply to feel all ready for the second ; and then when he lifted the second it gave him the impression of heaviness or lightness. If, under these conditions, the second weight felt light, he called it lighter than the first ;

if it felt heavy, he called it heavier than the first. If you, as experimenter, watched your subject's hands, you saw, sometimes at least, that the weight which seemed light came up quickly while one which seemed heavy came up with some lag. It seemed, then, that on lifting the first weight the subject got his hand adjusted for that weight, so that his second lift was just forcible enough to suit that first weight. If the second weight was lighter it came up easily and quickly and felt light, but if the second weight was heavier it lagged and felt heavy. The process appeared to employ muscular adjustment rather than mental images. Introspection, checked up by objective observation, had made an important discovery.

The introduction of this type of experiment is to be credited to Professor G. E. Müller of the University of Göttingen, more than to any other one psychologist. Müller, born in 1850, was one of a few German psychologists who, without being pupils of Wundt—being rivals, rather— had started laboratories not long after Wundt. This concept of a set or adjustment—in German, Einstellung— employed by Müller about 1890, has stuck, and still appears to be one of extreme value.

Müller went on to apply his new introspective method to the study of memory. The study of memory had just been effectively started by Ebbinghaus (1850–1909), another of the early experimentalists who were independent of Wundt. Ebbinghaus's now classical experiments on the curve of forgetting and on many other problems of memory had been purely objective. That is, his data consisted in records of how long it required to learn a certain lesson, or how long it required to relearn it after an interval. No introspective data were involved. Ebbinghaus had inter- preted his results along the lines of the association psycho- logy. Müller, apparently entertaining some doubt as to this interpretation, required his subjects not only to memorize and recall, but to report the experience of memorizing and of recalling. The subjects had a good deal of experience to report. They seemed to be very active during memorizing, and active in a variety of ways. They seemed to be very far from receiving the material passively and letting it associate itself together by some automatic process. Disconnected material, such as the lists of numbers or of nonsense syllables that are favourites in psychological laboratories, they heard in rhythmical form, or saw as if grouped into pairs and the like. They noted similarities and contrasts in the material, they lugged in meanings that tied different items together. Groupings, relations, and meanings were the keys to effective memorizing—such was the evidence of the introspective reports.

One of Müller's subjects in his later experiments—for he continued his study of memory for twenty or thirty years—was a certain Dr. X of the department of mathematics in the university. Dr. X was an arithmetical prodigy with a surprising memory for numbers. His memory span was enormous. What we call the memory span for digits is the longest list of one-place numbers that can be exactly repeated immediately after reading or hearing the list once through. You would have no trouble with a list of six digits, such as

$$8\ 3\ 6\ 9\ 2\ 7$$

so that your momory span for digits would be at least six. On the other hand, if you read the list

$$4\ 9\ 8\ 3\ 6\ 0\ 2\ 7\ 5\ 9$$

just once, and then try to repeat it from memory, you will agree that that is about your limit. The usual limit for young educated adults is seven, eight, or nine. But Dr. X, in similar tests, repeated lists of forty to fifty digits after one reading ; and Müller, as a psychologist, tried to discover how this feat was accomplished. Objective tests with other material showed that Dr. X's memory was not remarkable, except for numbers. Introspective reports indicated that he always grouped the numbers, grasping them as three-place numbers which he further combined into six-place numbers. Now every three-place number, to Dr. X, was like an old friend. He had studied them all and knew the characteristics of each one. He knew all the prime numbers up to one thousand, all the squares and cubes, and all other numbers with interesting arithmetical properties, just as you know the number 365 from its association with the year. The number 738, for example, being just 9 more than the cube of 9, would catch his attention instantly, and, as he said, 'of course could not be forgotten.' Dr. X's history was instructive. As a child he had taken a fancy to the house numbers along the street. All his boyhood he had played with numbers, ruminated over numbers, and discovered for himself many of their fascinating relationships. Thus for him, as an adult, to memorize a list of digits was a very different process from what it would be for most of us. And yet, as Müller found, most persons in memorizing do make use of such relationships, groupings, and meanings as they have ready for use. Memorizing is an active grasping process, and even the 'human sponge' is anything but a passive absorber. Thus Müller, by combining introspective with objective studies of memory, reached highly important results.

THOUGHT PROCESSES AS REVEALED BY INTROSPECTION

Instead of thinking of introspection as the old, original method of psychology, we have, it seems to me, to recognize that the beginnings of methodical introspection are to be found in this work of Müller and his pupils, starting about

1890. Titchener, always eager for any development of this sort, introduced the method into his laboratory at Cornell for the study of processes of comparison, about the year 1900. It was about the same time that another great psychologist, with whose name you are all familiar in other connexions, Alfred Binet of Paris (1857–1911), spontaneously hit upon the same method in attempting to study the process of thinking. In his early days, Binet had written a book on the psychology of reasoning, quite in the old style, without bothering to obtain any first-hand observations, but trusting to logic and the association doctrine to furnish a scheme of the process. At that time he had held that reasoning must be a play of images, a manipulation of images. About 1900 he took up the matter again, but based his conclusions on actual thinking processes reported by his two young daughters, thirteen and fourteen years old. He gave them little problems to solve and asked them to describe their processes or experiences during the solution. He would quiz them : ' Just how did you think of that object ? Did you see it ? Or say its name to yourself ? ' Sometimes his subjects reported images, but in a surprising number of instances they denied the presence of images, and Binet was thus forced to give up his view that thinking consisted necessarily in the manipulation of images. It seemed to him that thinking went on in terms of what he could find no better name for than just ' thoughts,' ' pensées.' The experience that you have in thinking of a thing consists in just thinking of it. Sometimes, to be sure, you see it ' in your mind's eye,' sometimes you name it, but often all you can say is that you are thinking of it. This may be regarded as a purely negative result, but at least it swept away the cobwebs of old schematization.

Independently of Binet, but probably influenced by the work of Müller, a group of German psychologists began about the same time a similar study of thought processes. This group centred about Külpe (1862–1915), a pupil of Wundt, professor at Würzburg and later at Bonn. For over ten years, and up to the time of the World War, he and his students devoted their efforts to this general problem.

First Marbe, a junior colleague of Külpe (born 1869, and now Külpe's successor at Würzburg), sought to describe the process of judging. He defined judgement as being any response of the subject that could be characterized as true or false. A judgement is a correct or incorrect answer to a question. Such is judgement as a performance, but Marbe wished to discover what it was as an experience. His procedure was to ask his subject a question, and when the subject answered to request him to review the experience of reaching the answer. He used simple questions, so as to have quick and easy processes of judgement, which he assumed would be easy to describe. But his result, on the main question, was rather negative. Often the subjects reported that the answer came automatically and that there was no experience to report. When they had something to report, it varied so much from one case to another that Marbe was forced to conclude against there being any single characteristic experience of judging.

But there was an interesting positive result that came out of this experiment. Often the subjects reported experiencing hesitancy, doubt, confidence in searching or approaching their answer ; and when they tried to describe these experiences in the conventional categories, sensation, image, and feeling, they found it impossible to do so. Marbe concluded that he had hit upon a type of experience that was new to psychology, and he gave it the impressive name, ' Bewusstseinslage,' or ' lay of consciousness,' the best English for which seems to be ' conscious attitude.'

When Marbe's experiment was repeated by Bühler (born

3

1879, now professor at Vienna) a few years later, with the difference that baffling questions were put to the subject instead of very simple ones, there was much more experience to report. In a variety of ingenious experiments, Bühler fully confirmed Marbe's conscious attitudes, and Binet's ' imageless thoughts,' as they may best be named in English.

Of other members of the Külpe group, I will mention two, Ach and Watt, who worked over the reaction time experiment, using the new introspective method, i.e. requiring their subject, after each reaction, to report his experience. Ach (born 1871, now Müller's successor at Göttingen) studied the simple reaction, which is a familiar experiment, since it is tried on the athletic field every time a foot race is started. There is a ready signal, at which the runners crouch for a forward spring, and then a pistol shot or other stimulus, on which they actually do spring forward with as little delay as possible. In the laboratory, a finger movement usually takes the place of the forward spring of the whole body, the stimulus may be a light or a sound, and the race is over as soon as an actual start has been made, for what is measured, in thousandths of a second, is the time elapsing between the stimulus and the first movement. A purely objective experiment so far ; but psychologists had naturally speculated as to what processes went on between the stimulus and the response, and Wundt had said that ' evidently ' there was the perception of the stimulus followed by the will to move. Ach asked his subjects, as soon as they had reacted, to review and report the experience of reacting. His data showed that the will to move, the effort, the determination to move as quickly as possible, came *before* the stimulus and was part of the preparation for the stimulus. Given that preparation, the stimulus called out the reaction automatically, so that usually there was no experience to report from the reaction period itself. There was the experience of getting ready before the stimulus, and there might be experience of various sorts after the reaction, but during the reaction time itself, which lasts usually not over a fifth of a second, there was no experience that could be identified. We can readily believe the same to be true of the runner on the mark. At the ready signal he becomes tense and eager, his will is aroused to the full before the pistol shot and does not need to be aroused after the shot. If it did, that runner would be left behind at the start.

Watt (1879–1925, a Scots student in Külpe's laboratory, later professor at Glasgow) studied a more complex form of response, which we call the associative reaction. The stimulus is a word shown to the subject, and the response is a word spoken by him. In controlled association, such as Watt used, the response word has to stand in an assigned relation to the stimulus word. It may be required to be a synonym, or an opposite, a part of the whole thing named, a whole of which the part is named, a higher class, a lower class, a co-ordinate class, etc. In place of a simple ready signal, the experimenter sets the subject his task by saying, ' Give the opposite of,' ' Name a part of,' etc., and then after a brief interval, the experimenter presents the actual stimulus word, as ' north ' or ' house.' The subject's response must be governed both by the stimulus word and by the task assigned. If I should pronounce the word ' high ' as a stimulus, with no special task assigned, you would be free to jump in any direction, according to the relative frequency, recency, and vividness of your associations. Some of you might think, ' high ball,' though I hope not ; ' high church ' would be better, or ' high light,' or ' sky ' or ' mountain ' or ' aeroplane.' But if I had prepared you by assigning ' opposites ' as the task, you would all respond ' low ' without hesitation. The preparation operates very efficiently in such cases.

Watt sought for the *experience* that takes place during such associative reactions and he found, once more, that more experience was reported from the period of preparation than from the period of actual reaction. When the subject was new to this kind of experiment, the getting ready to give an opposite, or a higher class, might be quite an experience. He might run over instances of the kind required, or he might gesture it out to himself. If he succeeded in preparing himself adequately before the stimulus word came, and if the stimulus word were not too difficult, his response, would be nearly automatic. As he became used to the tasks, his preparation itself became more automatic and less of an experience.

Ach and Watt agreed on the importance of preparation for a reaction—preparation, adjustment, set, Einstellung we might call it, remembering Müller's similar discovery. If we let the passage of time be represented by a horizontal line extending from left to right, and if on that line we mark a point P to denote the preparatory signal, a point S to denote the stimulus, and a point R to denote the response, then the time P-S is called the fore period of the reaction, and the time S-R the main period. The fore period is the time of preparation and the main period the time of execution. What Ach and Watt demonstrated was that most of the effort and active experience—and doubtless most of the real work—was done in the fore period. We can think of the organism as typically ready for something rather than as in a neutral, passive state. Though

P . S R

FORE MAIN
periods

stimuli do sometimes surprise the organism, catching it in an unprepared state, most reactions are prepared for, the organism being already adjusted to the situation and, in some sense, anticipating the stimuli to which it responds. This fact of preparation, set, or Einstellung is a fact of prime importance in understanding behaviour. Undoubtedly, this line of facts is the most solid contribution of the Külpe group of investigators.

Of their other discoveries, the conscious attitudes have been generally accepted as representing a real fact of experience, though not necessarily an elementary fact. It is quite possible that the feeling or attitude of hesitancy, for example, is the feeling of a bodily attitude, and could be analysed into sensations of posture and muscular strain and movement. Later introspective work has indicated that such may be the case.

Imageless thought, the third major finding of the Külpe group, has come in for the most doubt and criticism. As a rough fact of experience it has often been confirmed. Regarded simply as a negative result, it has at least the value of showing that thinking does not consist in a play or manipulation of images. The objects thought of are not necessarily either pictured or named, and thought may be perfectly clear and definite with only the vaguest of images. But the imageless thought adherents were not content to take their results as purely negative, or merely as a mild corrective of the previously accepted system of mental chemistry, with its elementary sensations, images, and feelings. Some of them insisted that they had discovered a new element, or, better still, a whole new class of elements, the thought elements or the relation elements. Such a claim was sure to arouse the adherents of the old system, and to raise very sharply the question whether the new introspective method was sound, whether it was good enough to warrant radical conclusions from its findings. This discussion was very active about 1910, and had something to do with the definite emergence of several of our contemporary schools. Existentialism took definite shape by reacting against imageless thought. Many middle-of-the-roaders were sceptical and inclined to regard introspection as only a rough sort of observation, good within limits but not to be pressed too far or depended on for fine analysis. The behaviourists reacted by rejecting introspection altogether. The Gestalt psychologists held that the trouble lay in the effort to use introspection as an instrument of analysis, and proposed to give up mental chemistry altogether, sensory elements and thought elements alike. The imageless thought controversy was a parting of the ways in psychological theory.[1]

THE EXISTENTIAL SCHOOL OF INTROSPECTIVE PSYCHOLOGY

I have just spoken as if existentialism emerged about 1910, whereas, in fact, it dates back, in a sense, to Wundt, Mach, and Avenarius in the nineteenth century. In seeking to distinguish psychology from physics, both alike being based upon sense data obtained by human observers, these theorists hit upon the formula that physics considers the external reference of sensory experience, whereas psychology considers experience as belonging to the experiencing individual. One particular formula was that physics takes experiences as indicators of facts lying beyond themselves, while psychology considered the experiences just for themselves. Another formula was that

[1] I myself made similar studies, independently of those of the Külpe group, though almost simultaneously with them, and reached the same result. I found evidence of imageless thought, and have always remained convinced that it is a fact, though I would now grant to the Gestalt psychologists that no good purpose was served by speaking of a ' thought element.' To my mind, the imageless thought concept is not dead, but only dormant at the present time. It seems to me important for a dynamics of thinking as much as for a description of the experience of thinking.

physics relates the experienced facts to each other, while psychology related them to the experiencing individual. In any case, psychology was to be a science of the individual's experience, and as the fundamental aim of science is description, psychology aimed to describe the individual's experience. It aimed to analyse experiences, to compare and classify them, to arrange them in an orderly system. Experiences were to be studied as *existences*, as facts deserving of description, analysis, and classification just on their own account. In other words, existential psychology was to be interested in the individual as an experiencer and not as a performer. His experiences were to be of interest to the psychologist, not for the light they might throw on his performances—as Müller used introspective data for illuminating the process of memorizing —but as the essential object of study. The primary method of psychology was the method of impression, which seemed to reveal the elementary experiences of the individual, but the introspective method was looked to with some hope for descriptions of more complex experiences. The only question was whether introspection could be depended on to give a true picture of experiences.

In a formal sense, this existential psychology was defined back in the nineteenth century, but as a consistent working programme in the laboratory it may be said to date from the work of the Külpe group and from the reaction of Titchener and others to that work. Wundt, though a professed introspective psychologist, did not like the form introspection had taken in the Külpe laboratory. He said it was not scientific, or at least not worthy to be placed alongside of the standard type of scientific observation. Typically, the scientific observer is all ready and set for the particular fact he has to observe. He has his eye at the telescope ready to note the precise instant when the star crosses the hair line. Science puts no trust in incidental observations, which, indeed, psychology has shown to be unreliable. The method of impression is on a par with other scientific observation, since the subject's attention is directed in advance to the precise matter to be observed. In experiments on thinking, however, you cannot tell in advance what to look for, the process is so variable and unpredictable. You cannot tell which way thought will jump. You cannot very well set your subject the problem of remembering where Calcutta is, and ask him in advance please to notice whether he sees an image of the map of India as he is finding his answer. For the same reason, you cannot repeat an observation, because the thought process cannot be repeated ; the thinker cannot search for an answer that he already has in mind. Wundt concluded that introspective study of thinking in the laboratory held little promise of scientific results. The trouble was essentially this : whereas in the method of impression, as in most scientific observation, the observer has the single task of observing, in introspection he has a double task, for he must think, judge, memorize, and then turn around and observe his experience during this performance. He has to do something in order to have anything to introspect. The reply of Bühler to this criticism was that, actually and practically, the subject seemed to have little difficulty, and that the observations of different subjects agreed to a sufficient degree to justify some confidence.

Titchener (1867–1927), a pupil of Wundt and his leading exponent in America, was above all an enthusiastic introspectionist, and therefore hopeful of each new attempt to extend the use of introspection in psychology. But he could not accept imageless thought, and put his finger on a serious difficulty of the method, considered as a method of describing experience. When a person is reporting what has gone through his mind during the process of solving a problem, he is apt to use such expressions as : ' Then I thought of ' such and such an object, or ' Then I remembered that ' such and such was the case. Titchener urged that to tell what one is thinking about is not to describe one's experience while thinking. In ordinary life we use language to refer to objects and objective situations, rather than to describe our feelings, thoughts, and experiences. We look up and say, ' I see it is clearing off,' rather than, ' My visual field is mostly mottled grey but with a few irregular areas of blue.' Our habit of referring to objects is so ingrained that we cannot easily drop it when we try to describe our experiences in an introspective experiment. Our language habits betray us into an error of report which may be called the error of objective reference. We report what our thoughts refer to, instead of describing their content. This error of objective reference is essentially the same as what Titchener had called the ' stimulus error ' in the simpler experiments by the method of impression. Suppose you are lifting weights and say of such a one, ' It feels like a heavy weight '—or suppose you are smelling odours and say of one, ' It must be peppermint '— you are talking about objects which you judge to be present, but you are not describing the particular experience you are getting from them. The only way to escape from this error of objective reference is by prolonged training under criticism from a rigid introspectionist. The only suitable subject in an introspective experiment is a highly trained observer, and few indeed are the observers whose reports, as published in the writings of introspectionists, come up to Titchener's standard of genuine description of experience.

Let us notice here that ordinary introspections which any of us can make, like ' This reminded me of that, and that led to the desired answer,' do reveal something of the course of a thinking process, even if they are of no service in a minute analysis of experience. They help in studying the performance of thinking, if not in analysing the experience of thinking. It is curious that introspection should be found of greater service to the psychology of performance than to the psychology of experience. Existential psychology, as championed by Titchener, does not care about performance but only about experience. Without denying the importance of studying performance, it leaves that study to others, in the belief that progress for pure psychology depends on limiting its attention to the description of experience. Existential psychology seeks to forget meanings and values and all reference to anything beyond the experience that is being described. Titchener believes that existential psychology is the only brand that can take its place as a pure science alongside of physics and biology, which also, in their respective fields, are first of all concerned to see what is there.

Existential psychology at the present time is rather an ideal or a programme for investigation, than anything like a rounded body of knowledge. It has the results of the method of impression, considered, however, not for the light they throw on the senses and on the mechanism of sensation, but simply as elementary sorts of experience. It works from sensation out, endeavouring to identify the sensory elements that are bound up in complex total experiences. If its discussions seem somewhat esoteric, the reply of the existentialist is that the same is true of inside work in physics or in any science that disregards everyday meanings and practical values in order to come to close quarters with the real facts of nature. But it seems to be something of a strain even for the most conscientious existentialist to maintain his aloofness from the individual as a performer. He seems almost relieved to admit the psychology of performance to his immediate neighbourhood as at least a closely related line of study. So, while the behaviourist will have naught of existential psychology nor admit for a moment its claims to be a real science, the existentialist has nothing worse to say of behaviourism than that it is not psychology in the least, but, rather, a bit of physiology.

CHAPTER III

BEHAVIOURISM

W E may best centre our study of behaviourism
around John B. Watson, leaving his antecedents
till we have seen what he meant by the new term
that he introduced. Behaviourism must be, by definition, what he teaches—or the essentials of what he teaches—
and other psychologists are entitled to be called behaviourists only so far as they agree with him. Inasmuch as
nearly every psychologist maintains some independence
of thought, the number of pure and unqualified behaviourists is limited ; but there are many who follow
Watson to a large extent, and many more whose views have
been much influenced by him. Moreover, behaviourism
has spread outside of the bounds of psychology into
sociology and elsewhere, sometimes appearing almost like a
religion or popular movement, with the result that a mere
psychologist has no special claim to know what behaviourism is, in all its ramifications.

WATSON'S BEHAVIOURISM

Born in 1878, Watson began his psychological career at
the University of Chicago and continued it at Johns
Hopkins, working energetically at animal and later at
child psychology. Revolt against the existing order in
psychology had been long smouldering within him, and in
1912, as he says,[1] ' the behaviourists reached the conclusion that they could no longer be content to work with

[1] J. B. Watson, *Behaviourism* (Routledge, 1924), p. 6.

intangibles and unapproachables. They decided either to give up psychology or else make it a natural science.' All that had been achieved by Wundt and the other experimentalists in their effort to make psychology a science amounted in Watson's eyes to the substitution of the word 'consciousness' for the 'soul' of medieval philosophy, merely replacing one intangible by another. In his book entitled *Behaviour : An Introduction to Comparative Psychology*, published in 1914, Watson defined his aim as follows :

Psychology as the behaviourist views it is a purely objective experimental branch of natural science. Its theoretical goal is the prediction and control of behaviour. Introspection forms no essential part of its methods, nor is the scientific value of its data dependent upon the readiness with which they lend themselves to interpretation in terms of consciousness. . . . The time seems to have come when psychology must discard all reference to consciousness ; when it need no longer delude itself into thinking that it is making mental states the object of observation. . . . It is possible to write a psychology, to define it as Pillsbury does (as the ' science of behaviour '), and never go back upon the definition : never to use the terms consciousness, mental states, mind, content, will, imagery, and the like. . . . It can be done in terms of stimulus and response, in terms of habit formation, habit integration, and the like. . . . In the main, the desire in all such work is to gain an accurate knowledge of adjustments and the stimuli calling them forth. The reason for this is to learn general and particular methods by which behaviour may be controlled. . . . If psychology would follow the plan suggested, the educator, the physician, the jurist, and the business man could utilize the data in a practical way, as soon as it could be experimentally obtained. Those who have occasion to apply psychological principles practically would find no need to complain as they do at the present time.

What makes us hopeful that the behaviourist's position is a defensible one is the fact that those branches of psychology which have already partially withdrawn from the parent, experimental psychology, and which are consequently less

dependent upon introspection, are to-day in a most flourishing
condition. Experimental pedagogy, the psychology of drugs,
the psychology of advertising, legal psychology, the psychology
of tests, and psychopathology are all vigorous growths. . . .
The only fault to be found with these disciplines is that much
of their material is now stated in terms of introspection,
whereas a statement in terms of objective results would be far
more valuable. . . . If this is done, work . . . on the human
being will be directly comparable with the work on animals.

As you can judge from the last paragraph quoted,
behaviourism did not, like Minerva, spring full-grown from
the head of Jove, but had developed gradually in the
womb of psychology. Or, to change the figure, we may
say that the outbreak of behaviourism in 1912–14 had its
predisposing and its exciting causes, such as the psychiatrist distinguishes in tracing the origin of an attack of
insanity. The predisposing causes were the contributions
to behaviour study that had long been made by objective
methods and that were being made in increasing numbers.
The exciting causes were the ambiguous position of this
objective psychology under the accepted definition of
psychology, the slurs cast upon it by the introspectionists,
and similar annoyances which at that time beset the
animal psychologist, the test psychologist, or the laboratory
psychologist whose concern was with performance rather
than with experience. We shall better understand the
phenomenon called behaviourism if we permit ourselves
to go back a little way from 1912, and see the preparation
that was being made for this outbreak.

Psychology defined as the science of consciousness as
such—just ' as such '—had never been heartily accepted
by American psychologists, though they had formally
subscribed to the definition. They had clung in practice
to the older tradition, and were still interested in the
' workings of the mind '—in the performances or functions
of the individual, rather than in his experiences as such.

The three deans of American psychology, about 1910, were William James of Harvard, George Trumbull Ladd of Yale, and G. Stanley Hall of Clark University. Ladd wrote on the physiological mechanisms of mental life, Hall wrote on its development in the child and in the race, and James was regarded as the father of the then new ' functional psychology.' There was much controversy in those days between functional and ' structural ' psychology, the latter aiming at the description and analysis of consciousness, and the former aiming to show the part which consciousness played in the life of the individual. Functional psychology sought to discover what needs of the organism were met by sense perception, by mental images, by emotion, by thinking. Taking the evolutionary point of view, it tried to divine at what stage in the development of the race the need for each mental process had become pressing enough to lead to the emergence of that particular process. In a general way, the higher mental processes were held to meet the need for a wider and more flexible control of the environment. Thus, functional psychology aimed to give psychology a place in the general field of biological science.

Functional psychology was specially strong and enterprising at the University of Chicago, under John Dewey (born 1859) and J. R. Angell (born 1869), the latter [1] a pupil of James ; and it was this type of psychology in which Watson was trained at Chicago. To Watson, however, it seemed to go only half-way, and to remain an inconsistent compromise between the structural psychology and a truly biological science. He says : [2]

The last fifteen years have seen the growth of what is called functional psychology. . . . It is stated in words which

---

[1] The functional viewpoint is well represented by Angell's *Psychology : An Introductory Study of the Structure and Function of Human Consciousness* (Henry Holt & Co., 1904).

[2] *Behaviour* (Henry Holt & Co., 1914), p. 8.

seem to throw emphasis upon the biological significance of conscious processes rather than upon the analysis of conscious states into introspectively isolable elements. The difference between functional psychology and structural psychology, as the functionalists have so far stated the case, is unintelligible. The terms sensation, perception, affection, emotion, volition are used as much by the functionalist as by the structuralist.

Besides this attempt of the functionalists to revise the definition of psychology by lining it up with biology, there had been a large amount of objective experimental work by those who were interested in what I have been calling the psychology of performance. Watson alludes to some of it in the first quotation above, when he speaks of experimental pedagogy, the psychology of tests, etc. He leaves the impression that all such objective work was very recent, as well as being partially vitiated by introspection. Tests, completely objective and free from introspection, go back to Galton in about 1880. Objective study of the learning process was active in the nineties, and may be dated back to Ebbinghaus's celebrated study of memory in 1885, a purely objective study. But even Galton and Ebbinghaus are not entitled to rank as the originators of objective psychology, for still further back we find the purely objective beginnings of work on reaction time ; and much of the work on sense perception, carried on by the method of impression, can perfectly well be considered as an objective study of an individual's accuracy of observation. Thus the objective method was in use from the very beginnings of experimental psychology, and the amount of research carried on by this method, up to 1900 or 1912, was very large indeed. As we saw before, psychology was not at all limited in practice to the study of experience. The study of performance was in full swing, and even those psychologists who made great use of introspection, like Müller and Külpe, used it largely for the light it threw on performance.

PRE-BEHAVIOURISTIC TREND TOWARD AN OBJECTIVE DEFINITION OF PSYCHOLOGY

The performance psychology, though active in the laboratories, scarcely became articulate in the way of definition, as far as I know, till the time of Cattell's St. Louis address in 1904. Cattell (born 1860) was a pupil of Stanley Hall, but more specially of Wundt, in whose laboratory he worked for several years, later working with Galton for a time and becoming much interested in the development of tests for measuring the individual's performance in as many directions as possible. Cattell started the psychological laboratories at Pennsylvania and Columbia. Now a feature of the St. Louis World's Fair of 1904 was a congress of arts and sciences, in which each branch of knowledge was represented by a leading authority who undertook to give a definition of his subject ; and Cattell was designated to define psychology. I will quote from his address : [1]

We are told indeed in our introductory text-books that psychology is the science of mind and that mind and matter are the most diverse things in the world. . . . The distinction between mind and matter is one of the last words of a philosophy which does not yet exist, rather than an axiom of everyday experience on which preliminary definitions may be based. . . .

Further, I am not convinced that psychology should be limited to the study of consciousness as such, in so far as this can be set off from the physical world. . . . I admire the products of the Herbartian school and the ever-increasing acuteness of introspective analysis from Locke to Ward. All this forms an important chapter in modern psychology ; but the positive scientific results are small in quantity when

---

[1] J. M'K. Cattell, in *Popular Science Monthly*, vol. lxvi. 1904, pp. 176–86.

4

compared with the objective experimental work accomplished in the past fifty years. There is no conflict between introspective analysis and objective experiment—on the contrary, they should and do continually co-operate. But the rather widespread notion that there is no psychology apart from introspection is refuted by the brute argument of accomplished fact.

It seems to me that most of the research work that has been done by me or in my laboratory is nearly as independent of introspection as work in physics or in zoology. The time of mental processes, the accuracy of perception and movement, the range of consciousness, fatigue and practice, the motor accompaniments of thought, memory, the association of ideas, the perception of space, colour-vision, preferences, judgements, individual differences, the behaviour of animals and of children, these and other topics I have investigated without requiring the slightest introspection on the part of the subject or undertaking such on my own part during the course of the experiments. . . .

It is certainly difficult to penetrate by analogy into the consciousness of the lower animals, of savages and of children, but the study of their behaviour has already yielded much and promises much more. . . .

If I did not believe that psychology affected conduct and could be applied in useful ways, I should regard my occupation as nearer to that of the professional chess-player or sword-swallower than to that of the engineer or scientific physician. . . . I see no reason why the application of systematized knowledge to the control of human nature may not in the course of the present century accomplish results commensurate with the nineteenth-century applications of physical science to the material world.

If Watson ever noticed this pronouncement, he probably regarded it as too much of a compromise to suit him, since he was interested, not simply in promoting objective psychology, but in eliminating everything else. For the same reason, he attached no importance to the proposals of McDougall and Pillsbury within the next few years, to the effect that psychology should be defined as the science of behaviour. I will quote from these writers at some length, in the interest of doing justice to the psychological background out of which behaviourism emerged in 1912.

William McDougall will later appear before us as the leader of the purposivistic school. In his little book on *Physiological Psychology*, published [1] in 1905, he discusses the definition of psychology as follows :

Psychology may be best and most comprehensively defined as the positive science of the conduct of living creatures. . . . Psychology is more commonly defined as the science of mind, or as the science of mental or psychical processes, or of consciousness, or of individual experience. Such definitions are ambiguous, and without further elaboration are not sufficiently comprehensive. They express the aims of a psychologist who relies solely upon introspection, the observation and analysis of his own experience, and who unduly neglects the manifestations of mental life afforded by the conduct of his fellow-creatures. . . . To define psychology as the science of experience or of consciousness is therefore to exclude the study of these unconscious factors, whereas the definition stated above brings all these within the scope of psychology without excluding the study of any part of experience or element of consciousness, for all experience affects conduct.

In 1908, in his *Introduction to Social Psychology*,[2] a book which immediately stepped into favour and remained for many years in active use, McDougall continues his discussion :

Psychologists must cease to be content with the sterile and narrow conception of their science as the science of consciousness, and must boldly assert its claim to be the positive science of the mind in all its aspects and modes of functioning, or, as I would prefer to say, the positive science of conduct or behaviour. Psychology must not regard the introspective

[1] By J. M. Dent & Sons.
[2] Published by Methuen & Co., and by John W. Luce & Co.

description of the stream of consciousness as its whole task, but only as a preliminary part of its work. Such introspective description, such 'pure psychology,' can never constitute a science, or at least can never rise to the level of an explanatory science ; and it can never in itself be of any great value to the social sciences. The basis required by all of them is a comparative and physiological psychology relying largely on objective methods, the observation of the behaviour of men and of animals of all varieties under all possible conditions of health and disease. . . . Happily this more generous conception of psychology is beginning to prevail.

W. B. Pillsbury (born 1872), a pupil of Titchener, published in 1911 his *Essentials of Psychology*,[1] which immediately became to a large extent the standard text-book of psychology in American colleges. His definition was probably acceptable to many psychologists of the time.

Psychology has been defined as the 'science of consciousness,' or as the 'science of experience subjectively regarded.' Each of these definitions has advantages, but none is free from objection. . . . Mind is known from man's activities. Psychology may be most satisfactorily defined as the science of human behaviour.

Man may be treated as objectively as any physical phenomenon. He may be regarded only with reference to what he does. Viewed in this way the end of our science is to understand human action. The practical end is to determine upon what human capacity depends and, in the light of this knowledge, to discover means of increasing man's efficiency. . . .

Even if we regard the understanding of human behaviour as the ultimate end of psychology, consciousness must still play a very important part in our science. By consciousness we mean a man's awareness of his own acts and their antecedents. . . . Consciousness is at once an important means of understanding behaviour and an interesting object of investigation for itself. . . . At the present stage in the development of psychology, it seems best to subordinate consciousness

---

[1] Published by The Macmillan Co.

to behaviour. Psychology is the science of behaviour. Behaviour is to be studied through the consciousness of the individual and by external observation.

The suggestion that psychology be regarded as the science of human behaviour was apparently making considerable headway when behaviourism appeared on the scene. The term, behaviour, seemed broad enough to cover the work of the introspective psychologists as well as that of the objective workers. For is not seeing or hearing or imagining or desiring a way of behaving ? To behave is to be active in some way, and certainly seeing and the rest are activities of the organism. There is no antagonism between behaviour and consciousness, as if an animal must be unconscious in order to behave. No doubt behaviour is closer to performance than to experience ' as such,' but even the existentialist says he is studying experience ' in its dependence upon the individual,' which is much like saying ' as a part of the individual's behaviour.'

For Watson, however, behaviour and consciousness were mutually exclusive, and to define psychology as the science of behaviour meant making a radical departure and ruling out all introspection, all reference to consciousness, and, as he conceived, practically all of psychology as it had developed up to 1912. To show why he saw the matter in that light we need to remember that he had specialized in animal psychology, and we need once more to go back a few years and trace the development of that study.

THORNDIKE AND THE RAPID GROWTH OF ANIMAL PSYCHOLOGY

Though animal behaviour had been of great interest to the biologist from the time of Darwin, we may safely credit Thorndike with its introduction into the psychological laboratory. Thorndike (born 1874), though a devoted pupil of both James and Cattell, was himself responsible for the idea of experimenting on animal instinct and learning. He showed, for example, that a newly hatched chick, placed upon a low box, would jump to the ground without hesitation; if placed on a box a few inches high, with hesitation; but if placed on a box a foot high, not at all. Thus the chick responded to distance, to the third dimension, without having had any opportunity to learn this response. As apparatus for the study of animal learning, Thorndike used mazes and trick cages or ' puzzle boxes.' If he took a chick away from the rest of the brood and placed it in a small enclosure, allowing only a circuitous route of escape, the chick ran around inside, peeping, going hither and thither, and finally getting out and rejoining the brood. Repeatedly placed back in the enclosure, the chick came by degrees to escape more quickly, till after a few trials he would dart at once along the open path. A hungry kitten placed in a cage with food close outside would push, claw, and bite everything within reach, including sooner or later the latch which opened the door ; replaced again and again, it gradually came to omit all useless movements and to operate the latch promptly and surely. Beginning in 1896, and continuing for a few years till his energies were absorbed in educational psychology, Thorndike applied his methods to chicks, fishes, dogs, and cats, and finally monkeys ; and this novel line of psychological work was immediately taken up by several leading American laboratories, with Yerkes, Watson, and others specializing in it. The animal was found to be a very convenient subject for experiments on learning, and the results threw light on human as well as animal learning.

In interpreting his results, Thorndike laid out the possibilities as follows : the animals might use ideas, either in reasoning or merely in association, or they might learn blindly by trial and error. Reasoning he believed to be ruled out by the gradualness of the animal's learning. The ' learning curves ' showed a gradual though irregular improvement, with no indications of sudden transition from not knowing the answer to knowing it. But if the animal had reasoned out the problem, he would have reached the solution at some particular time, and after that would know the answer and always do the right thing promptly. Thorndike concluded that his animals did not learn by reasoning. Whether they made any use of ideas at all, he could not certainly determine, but he inclined to think not. Learning by imitation he excluded by definite experimental evidence : neither cats nor monkeys derived any appreciable advantage from having a trick performed for them by an animal that had already mastered it. Thorndike was left with trial and error as the only possibility. The animals learned not by watching, not by considering, but by doing. They went through a variety of motor responses to the situation, and by some blind, gradual process the unsuccessful responses were eliminated and the successful response strengthened and firmly attached to the situation. Trial and error was the animal method of learning.

Human beings, of course, use ideas ; but Thorndike pointed out that trial and error learning is by no means confined to animals. Motor skill, as in tennis, he thought was acquired not by rational consideration or by insight, but by varied motor performance, with stamping out of unsuccessful and stamping in of the successful variants of response. Moreover, brute learning, he believed, was the basis for the development of ideas and reasoning. Man is superior to the animals fundamentally because he has more power of brute learning. He learns rapidly and learns many responses and so wins a basis for thinking.

Thorndike conceived of learning as a process of establishing bonds or connexions in the nervous system between the incoming nerves excited by the stimulus and the motor nerves which aroused the muscles and so gave the motor response. He believed that the laws of this learning mechanism could be reduced to two : the law of exercise, namely, that bonds are strengthened by use and weakened by prolonged disuse ; and the law of effect, namely, that those bonds are strengthened, or gain the advantage over others, which lead to a satisfactory issue of the situation. When the activity of one brain mechanism results in pleasure or satisfaction to the animal, that mechanism is thereby strengthened. When the operation of another brain mechanism yields discomfort to the animal, that mechanism is thereby weakened. If we understood the inner physiology of satisfaction and discomfort, we should see how they strengthen or weaken the brain mechanisms that have just been active and that are accordingly specially affected by these physiological conditions. We know little of the physiology of satisfaction and discomfort, but we absolutely need the law of effect as a first approximation to the ultimate law that will explain why the unsuccessful reactions are eliminated and the successful reaction firmly attached to the situation, in trial and error learning.

I have not attempted to indicate how much of Thorndike's theory was strictly original. In its main lines it was in accordance with the association doctrine. But Thorndike was speaking of connexions formed between stimulus and motor response rather than between one idea and another; and, most important, he had his experimental evidence to support his views. He seemed to many, in 1900, a dangerous radical, both in his view of animal behaviour and in his conception of human mentality. As time went on, the animal psychologists who followed tried to go one better in radicalism and especially tried to simplify the theory of learning by getting rid of the law of effect.

Thorndike's own researches in educational psychology were as objective in method as those in animal psychology ; and his thinking inclined him more and more to stress behaviour as at least one of the great objects of psychological study. In 1905, to be sure, he defines psychology in terms primarily of consciousness :

The world is made up of physical and mental facts. . . . Psychology . . . deals with the latter. . . . Since the majority of human actions are directly connected with thoughts and feelings, psychology deals with not only the mental states, but also the acts or conduct of men.[1]

In 1911, however, he devotes a chapter to discussing the relative merits of ' The Study of Consciousness and the Study of Behaviour,' and comes out strongly for a behaviour psychology :

The statements about human nature made by psychologists are of two sorts—statements about consciousness . . . and statements about behaviour. . . .

On the whole, the psychological work of the last quarter of the nineteenth century emphasized the study of consciousness. . . . There was a tendency to an unwise, if not bigoted, attempt to make the science of human nature synonymous with the science of facts revealed by introspection. . . .

The studies reprinted in this volume [i.e. his original studies of animal learning and instinct] produced in their author an increased respect for psychology as the science of behaviour. . . . Psychology may be, at least in part, as independent of introspection as physics is. Behaviour includes consciousness *and* action, states of mind *and* their connexions.[2]

[1] E. L. Thorndike, *Elements of Psychology* (Routledge, 1905), pp. 1, 10.
[2] E. L. Thorndike, *Animal Intelligence : Experimental Studies* (Macmillan, 1911), pp. 1–5, 15.

WHY BEHAVIOURISM CAME AS A REVOLT AND NOT AS A PEACEFUL DEVELOPMENT

From all that has been said, it is clear enough that be-haviourism was well prepared for, both in the practice of the laboratories and in the new efforts at definition made by several leading psychologists in the first decade of the century. The rapid and interesting development of animal psychology, in particular, was one of the important pre-disposing causes for the outbreak of behaviourism.

But the ' exciting cause ' was the repressive attitude toward animal psychology assumed by those important psychologists of that day who were perfectly clear that psychology was, and must logically be, the study of conscious experience and nothing else. From this major premise they reasoned logically that behaviour data were not psychology at all unless translated over into terms of the animal's consciousness. Now since the days of Descartes it had been recognized that you cannot prove conscious-ness in animals. Shall we assume that all animals, down to the very lowest, are conscious in their behaviour, or shall we limit consciousness to animals that learn, or to animals that have a nervous system, or by what criterion shall we draw the line ? At best, inference from behaviour to consciousness in animals was reasoning by analogy and a leap in the dark. Titchener and others granted that some such inferences might legitimately be drawn, provided caution were used, and that thus animal experiments could throw some light on psychology. But as this leap in the dark was necessary in order to make any psychological use of the behaviour data, animal psychology was at best an indirect and relatively unimportant part of our science.

Meanwhile the animal psychologists were obtaining objective results on such problems as instinct and learning,

and disliked to be told they must resort to dubious analogies
in order to make psychology out of their findings. Probably many of them chafed under the dictum of the orthodox psychologist, and Watson, being the most aggressive,
did not chafe in silence. He retorted, in effect, ' Show me
any results of your vaunted introspection that can bear
comparison with the objective results of an animal experiment,' and, without waiting for an answer, he went on to
say that the animal psychologists were, as matters stood,
the only group who were doing really scientific work in
psychology, and that human psychology should take a
leaf out of their book, give up introspection, and devote
itself exclusively to objective behaviour study. He pointed
his accusing finger at the imageless thought controversy
and at other recent and still debated findings of the introspectionists, and concluded that psychology would remain
a debating society and not a science until introspection
was discarded.

Watson's objection to introspection was not grounded
chiefly on the difficulties of this type of observation, such
as had been pointed out by Wundt and Titchener. It
seemed to him that the introspectionist pretended to
observe something immaterial and outside of the realm of
natural phenomena. Wundt and Titchener had, to be
sure, expressly disclaimed any such pretension, in saying
that the raw data of observation were the same for physics
and for psychology ; but to Watson introspection was all
tangled up with consciousness as a mere verbal substitute
for the soul. He admitted, a little later,[1] that one could
observe one's own behaviour and report, ' for example,
that I am writing, that my face is flushed, etc.,' and he
did not rule out the use of this verbal report method in
experiments on the senses. Only, verbal report must not

[1] *Psychology from the Standpoint of a Behaviourist* (J. B. Lippincott
Co., 1919), p. 39.

be construed as revealing consciousness. Consciousness itself he does not seriously object to, except in the ' psychological sense.' [1] It was only the consciousness which the psychologist pretended to observe by introspection that was so objectionable.

Watson denied the existence of consciousness 'in a psychological sense,' and with it went sensation, feeling and image, long regarded as the elements of conscious experience. The word sensation he scrupulously avoids in his treatment of the senses, using instead such expressions as 'response to light,' 'auditory response,' 'olfactory response.' He even includes the after-image in his treatment. Thus he says : [2]

One of the most interesting sets of phenomena to be met with in the whole of sensory physiology appears in the after-effects of monochromatic light stimulation. After the eye has been stimulated for a time by a monochromatic light which is then removed, one of two things may be reported by the subject : The subject may react as though he were stimulated anew by the original light, the so-called ' positive after-image ' ; or, as though he were stimulated by light . . . complementary to the original light, the 'negative after-image.' We can illustrate this by data obtained by the verbal report method. If we stimulate with . . . blue and the subject then looks at a grey screen, he will say, ' I see yellow.'

Thus the behaviourist was able to take over into his psychology all the results of the method of impression applied to the senses.

Watson was specially anxious to disprove the claims of memory images and of feelings to be regarded as facts. He endeavoured to show [3] that the so-called memory images which most people believed themselves to have con-

[1] *Behaviour*, 1914, p. 27.

[2] *Psychology from the Standpoint of a Behaviourist*, 1919, p. 61.

[3] *Behaviour*, 1914, p. 16.

sisted partly in kinesthetic 'impulses' (sensations) and partly in verbal responses of the subject, and that the feelings of pleasantness and unpleasantness were partly sensory impulses from the sex organs or other erogenous zones, and partly incipient movements of approach or escape. Neither image nor feeling was 'centrally aroused,' i.e. originating in the brain and so distinct from stimulus-response behaviour. All behaviour was sensorimotor, consisting of stimulus-response units, each of which began with a stimulus to some sense organ and terminated in a muscular or glandular response. The nervous system functioned in complete arcs. The brain must not be overstressed or made a fetish. Psychologists had fallen into the habit of devoting considerable attention to the brain, but the behaviourist held that in doing so they had isolated it from the rest of the body and made it just another substitute for the soul. They had supposed the brain to be the organ of memory and thought, and so made of these purely 'central' processes distinct from sensorimotor behaviour, accessible only to introspection and not to the objective methods of behaviour study.

Now behaviour, Watson continued, was not always readily observed from without. It was not always overt or 'explicit,' but might be internal or 'implicit.' Visceral behaviour was implicit because it was so hidden in the interior. Inner speech, consisting, as he thought, of little speech movements, was implicit because the movements were too slight to be observed by the unaided eye or ear. The line of advance in the study of the extremely important implicit behaviour was to perfect our recording apparatus. Behaviour consisted in instinctive or unlearned responses, and in habits or learned responses, and either learned or unlearned responses might be explicit or implicit. A large share of the task of behaviouristic psychology would be to trace the individual's development of explicit and implicit habits ; and knowledge so gained could be applied to the control and improvement of human behaviour.

Behaviourism, in 1912–14, was a ' youth movement.' Watson was a young man, and his followers were mostly in the younger generation. They felt that Watson was changing the atmosphere of psychology, by clearing away old mysteries, uncertainties, complexities, and difficulties, which were a heritage from philosophy, and which the older psychologists had not been able to shake off. In their enthusiasm they exaggerated the revolution. I remember a student who came from one of the behaviourists to Columbia—to Cattell's laboratory, if you please—and said he knew that our laboratory was wholly given up to introspection and consequently was of no use to him, but that he planned to work in the zoological laboratory, and would like to have the use of our shop for constructing his apparatus. The actual revolution in psychological research was slight. Objective work continued ; introspective work continued. Before tracing the further development of American behaviourism, and before mentioning other prominent contributors to this development, we must go back again and consider some important happenings in Russia, which were scarcely known in America prior to 1912, but which later proved of the greatest importance to behaviourism.

RUSSIAN OBJECTIVISM AND THE CONDITIONED REFLEX

Behaviourism in America started as a protest rather than as a discovery. The Russian work which we are now to consider started with the discovery of the conditioned reflex, and that discovery has been of more aid and comfort to our behaviourists than any single result of their own.

It was about 1905 that the conditioned reflex was discovered almost simultaneously in two laboratories in what was then known as St. Petersburg.[1] We need not go into the question of priority between the two discoverers, Pavlov and Bechterev, the first a physiologist, the other a neurologist. The two were rivals in this work and stimulated each other to great activity. As we shall have more to say of Pavlov, let us begin with Bechterev.

Bechterev (1857–1927) had been working with great energy since about 1880 on the anatomy and pathology of the nervous system, on reflexes, and on nervous and mental diseases. His studies led him to the conception of what he called associated reflexes, the same thing that Pavlov called conditioned reflexes. Bechterev, however, was working with motor reflexes, Pavlov with glandular or secretory reflexes. What Bechterev noticed was something like this : If cold is applied to the skin, there is a catching of the breath, a natural reflex. If another stimulus which by itself has no marked effect on breathing is applied repeatedly along with the cold on the skin, that other stimulus in time will come to have the same effect. This, then, was a learned or associated reflex. Bechterev and his students worked assiduously on the problem thus opened up. They worked on human as well as animal subjects. They worked on mentally disordered subjects, in the hope of throwing light upon the neuroses and psychoses and of building up an objective approach to psychiatry. Bechterev wrote books on his discoveries and theories, under the names of ' objective psychology ' and ' reflexology.' Without disputing the legitimacy of introspective psychology, he proposed to see how far he could

[1] It was also discovered independently and simultaneously by E. B. Twitmyer at the University of Pennsylvania.

go on a purely objective basis, using the reflex as his fundamental concept, and he believed that he was able to cover the psychological subject-matter quite completely without introducing any such terms as sensation, feeling, or thought. His book on *Objective Psychology* was first published in Russian in 1907, and translated into German in 1913.

Pavlov (born 1849) started to study for the priesthood but was deflected into medicine and thence into physiology. He worked for many years on the physiology of digestion and made some highly ingenious and instructive experiments. Soon after 1900, while working on this subject, he noticed a peculiar fact in the behaviour of the dog that he was using as subject. He had arranged apparatus for collecting the dog's saliva directly from one of the salivary glands, and was giving the animal food to arouse the flow of saliva. He noticed that the saliva began to flow in an experienced dog before the food was actually placed in his mouth. It flowed at the sight of the dish containing the food, or at the approach of the attendant who customarily brought the food, or even at the sound of the attendant's footsteps in the adjoining room. Now while food in the mouth is undoubtedly a natural stimulus for the reflex flow of saliva, the sight of a person or the sound of his footsteps can hardly be a natural stimulus for this response, but must have become attached to the response in the course of the prolonged experiment, so as to serve as a preliminary signal. Pavlov saw that the capacity for acquiring such signals must be very important in the development of an individual animal's adaptation to his particular environment. He saw also that he had struck a promising lead toward the experimental study of the higher brain functions, and proceeded to turn the energies of his laboratory in that direction. In the course of twenty-five years, hundreds of articles and doctoral dissertations on various ramifications of this problem were issued from his laboratory. He coined the term, conditioned reflex, to stand for a reflex in which the response had become attached to some substitute for the natural stimulus.

The first step was to discover how a reflex could become conditioned. He experimented to see whether he could attach the salivary response to the sound of a buzzer or of a metronome. He let the metronome tick for a minute and then put food in a dog's mouth ; waited fifteen minutes, started the metronome again and after a minute again fed the dog. After this procedure had been gone through a number of times, the saliva began to flow before the end of the minute, anticipating the food stimulus. If the food stimulus was then omitted, a good flow of saliva would nevertheless be obtained. But if the experiment continued on this line, the metronome being sounded for a minute, but the food not being given at the end of that time, the flow of saliva diminished from trial to trial, and after a few such trials the conditioned reflex which had been established was extinguished.

Now suppose the conditioned reflex had been established and the experiment was then discontinued till the following day. On the first trial the metronome gave no response ; but the number of trials (metronome always followed by food) required to establish the reflex on the second day was less than on the first day ; and if the conditioning experiment, without extinction, was repeated day after day, the time soon came when the conditioned reflex held over from day to day. If the extinguishing procedure—metronome with no food—were applied to such a thoroughly established reflex, the extinction was not so rapid and was only temporary, since the conditioned response would appear at once on the next day. Yet if the extinguishing procedure were applied repeatedly on a

5

series of days, it finally eradicated the conditioned reflex.

The processes of establishment and of extinction of a conditioned reflex were so closely parallel that Pavlov concluded the brain mechanisms were the same, except that in one case a positive response was being conditioned, and in the other a negative or inhibitory response.

Of the many other variations of the experiment that were tried in Pavlov's laboratory, I will mention the rather complicated and laborious one on ' differentiation,' which means the establishment of a positive conditioned reflex to one stimulus along with absence of response to another similar stimulus. He was interested to see how far he could push the animal in the direction of fine differentiation. He found that differentiation could be established between two tuning-fork tones differing by less than a semitone of the musical scale. The process was as follows. First he used a single tone, say middle C, always following it by the food stimulus. When positive response to middle C was well established, he commenced sounding another, much higher tone. At the first sounding of this new tone, the saliva flows as before, the reflex carries over to this similar stimulus. But the high tone is not followed by food. Whenever the lower tone is sounded, food follows ; but when the higher tone is sounded, there is no food. By repeating this procedure sufficiently, he could extinguish the salivary response to the higher tone, while leaving it intact to the lower tone. The third stage of the experiment now begins, and consists in bringing the upper tone down toward the lower, day by day, a little closer, taking care not to disturb the differentiation which has been established. It may take many months to get the two tones down to only a note apart, with differentiation undisturbed ; but the claim is made that this has been achieved in some animals. If the attempt is made to push the animal beyond his limit, he may lose all the conditioned responses that have been established, and become practically a neurotic dog, so the experimenters say.

It should be said that such results demand confirmation in another laboratory than the one in which they were first obtained. There are pitfalls in such work ; especially there is the chance that the animal is responding to the experimenter and his movements and unconscious expressions, and not at all to the stimuli which the experimenter is intentionally applying. In view of this danger, Pavlov drew plans for a special conditioned reflex laboratory, with elaborate provisions for keeping the experimenter out of the dog's sight and hearing, and for eliminating distracting sights and sounds from outside. The Russian Government has recently built this laboratory for him, and he is now engaged in repeating his earlier experiments with the precautions thus made possible. But the establishment and extinction of conditioned reflexes, at least, have been abundantly confirmed by other experimenters.

From all his results,[1] vivified by an active imagination Pavlov has reached a theory of the functions of the brain. It has, he believes, two inclusive functions. On the sensory side, it consists of analysers which pick out particular stimuli from the mass of physical motions constantly impinging on the organism. In this function it is analogous to a radio receiving set. On the motor side, the brain function consists of conditioned reflexes. All learned behaviour, even the complex behaviour of man, consists of conditioned reflexes. That conditioning is a function of the cerebrum is indicated by the result of injuries to this part of the brain, which make it impossible

[1] I. P. Pavlov, *Conditioned Reflexes*, translated by G. V. Anrep (Oxford University Press, 1927); *Lectures on Conditioned Reflexes*, translated by W. H. Gantt (International Publishers Co., 1928).

to condition the animal. Sleep, also, prevents conditioning ; so that this process depends on activity of the cerebrum.

Pavlov, then, calls his work brain physiology. He makes no claim to be a psychologist ; in fact, that is about the last thing he would claim. Time and again, in lecturing on his results, he has closed with some such expression as the following :

In conclusion, we must count it an uncontested fact that the physiology of the highest part of the nervous system of higher animals cannot be successfully studied unless we utterly renounce the untenable pretensions of psychology.

When he asked his psychological colleagues what set of concepts they would use in explaining his conditioned reflexes, they suggested desire, expectation, disappointment, and the like ; but these he found he could not use for predicting what would happen or devising new forms of experiment. When he used his physiological concepts, reinforcement, inhibition, and the like, he was led on fruitfully. So he concluded that the key to the understanding of behaviour lies wholly with physiology. It is true, however, that when he became acquainted with Thorndike's experiments on animal learning, he greeted them as quite pertinent to his own line of study.

In view of his general opposition to psychology, it is curious to note that Pavlov's work has aroused more interest among psychologists than among physiologists. One of his best friends among the physiologists wrote him that he hoped he would drop this conditioned reflex work and get back to genuine physiology. On the other hand, psychologists have received the conditioned reflex with open arms ; and the behaviourists especially found in it a great contribution.

WATSON'S LATER DEVELOPMENT

Only gradually did the conditioned reflex make itself felt in American behaviourism. Watson, in 1914, mentions Pavlov's methods as available for experimentation on animals, though rather inferior to other methods. Very soon, however, he was impressed by the complete objectivity of the conditioned reflex type of experimentation, as practised by Bechterev as well as by Pavlov, and suggested that it should be substituted for the verbal report method which at the best was somewhat akin to introspection. In 1919, he gives it an honourable place in his list of psychological methods for use on human as well as on animal subjects, and also makes use of the conditioned reflex concept in his discussion of emotions, pointing out that ' the fear reactions we see in the dark, in graveyards at night, at lightning, and in many other definite situations, probably belong in the conditioned emotional reaction class.' [1] By 1924 he has come to entertain the hypothesis that the conditioned reflex affords the key to all habit formation, including the integration of simple movements into complex learned acts ; but he is not fully convinced in this matter.[2] Meanwhile Smith and Guthrie had proposed, in a book with decided behaviouristic leanings,[3] to regard all learning as based upon the conditioned reflex.

It will be recalled that Thorndike had believed it necessary, in order to account for trial and error learning, to formulate a ' law of effect.' Successful responses to a situation, by yielding satisfaction to the animal, were gradually stamped in, while the unsuccessful were stamped

[1] *Psychology from the Standpoint of a Behaviourist*, 1919, p. 213.
[2] *Behaviourism*, 1924, pp. 24, 25, 163, 166–9.
[3] S. Smith and E. R. Guthrie, *General Psychology in Terms of Behaviour* (Appleton, 1921).

out by the discomfort of failure. Although satisfaction and discomfort could be thought of as physiological states, and although Watson himself had suggested how they might be conceived in behavioural terms,[1] yet the law of effect seemed from its wording to assume conscious states of feeling in the animal and even to allow them to operate as causal factors in behaviour. Therefore the behaviourists have sought to eliminate the law of effect, by reduction of it to the law of exercise or by other means. Watson at first pinned his faith upon the long-accepted laws of frequency and recency, which may be regarded as sub-laws under the law of exercise. He pointed out that an animal learning to run a maze is bound to take the correct path at least once on every trial, before he can escape, whereas any particular blind alley may be skipped on some trials. Thus the successful response will gradually acquire a balance of greater frequency over the unsuccess-ful. Thorndike, in reply, pointed out that an unsuccessful response was often repeated several times during the same trial, and might as a matter of count have a balance of frequency in its favour even up to the time when the correct response was well 'stamped in.' So this round of the contest seemed to result in a draw. Later, when the conditioned reflex came into view, it was adopted as a sufficient weapon against the law of effect. But it must be admitted that trial and error learning presents a difficult problem, requiring more than merely verbal solution ; and much varied work is being done upon it by psycholo-gists generally and quite apart from its bearing upon the merits of behaviourism.

At the first dawn of behaviourism, it had been derided as 'muscle twitch psychology,' and as nothing more nor less than a little piece of physiology. Watson combated this criticism energetically, and I think successfully, by

[1] See above, p. 61.

explaining that the behaviourist, though interested in motor behaviour, took it as the activity of the whole individual, whereas physiology was characteristically concerned with the various organs composing the individual. But it certainly seemed that the scope of behaviourism was bound to be more limited than that of psychology, since sensation, perception, memory, thinking, emotion, and desire were to be excluded. The admission of the verbal report method, along with care in the use of words, saved the day for sensation, and probably for perception, though it must be said that behaviourists have neglected the latter highly important topic.

Memory seems to have caused the behaviourists more trouble than was necessary. Even as late as 1924, we find Watson beginning a discussion of memory with the statement that ' The behaviourist never uses the term " memory." He believes that it has no place in an objective psychology,' and then proceeding to use the word freely in quotation marks, while discussing the retention of skill and of facts, finally coming out with the statement that ' memory in the behaviourist's sense is any exhibition of manual, verbal, or visceral organization put on prior to the time of the test.' The feeling of familiarity, or the ' warmth and intimacy ' which in James's description cling about true memory, simply mean revival of old visceral (emotional) responses.[1]

Implicit behaviour saved the day for thinking and emotion. Thinking could be included under behaviour by supposing it to consist of implicit speech reactions or subvocal talking, and emotion by supposing it to consist of implicit visceral reactions. Thus, while sensation and

[1] *Behaviourism*, 1924, pp. 177, 190, 212. The revised edition of 1930 (W. W. Norton & Co., publishers) indicates no serious change in Watson's views on memory or on the other matters for which we have taken the first edition as our source of information.

memory were taken into behaviour simply by speaking of them in behaviour terms, thinking and emotion required definite hypotheses which are susceptible to experimental check.

Watson's hypothesis as to thinking is, in general, that it must be a sensorimotor performance of some sort, and that it is implicit, since admittedly one's thoughts are often not betrayed by visible movements or by audible speech. Thinking is implicit behaviour that is substituted for overt manipulation. We become conditioned to name objects and actions. The child often says what he is doing as he does it. Two steps from that stage bring the child to a stage in which his talking to himself (1) is inaudible, and (2) occurs when he is not actually manipulating but only, as we say, thinking about doing so. Subvocal talking is often substituted for actual manipulation in the process of solving a practical problem, with resulting economy of time and effort. Instead of moving the piano bodily to a new position in the room, to see how it looks there, we say to ourselves, 'Suppose I moved the piano over there,' and continue, 'But it would jut out over the window. That won't do.' It appeared probable to Watson, then, that the particular implicit behaviour that got substituted for actual manipulation consisted mostly of speech movements.

This hypothesis may come out more clearly if we contrast it with a somewhat broader hypothesis advanced by Hollingworth.[1] He defines thought as the use in problem solution of substitutes or symbols for the real objects and processes that enter into the problem. Often the symbol is a word, sometimes it is a mathematical symbol, sometimes it is a diagram representing the situation, sometimes it is a mental image, and sometimes it is an actual object

[1] H. L. Hollingworth, *The Psychology of Thought* (Appleton, 1926), pp. 4, 11.

that is taken to represent the object thought about. A general, in planning an operation, or in following a battle as it develops, may do his thinking over a map, with flags on pins stuck into the map to designate the different regiments in their positions. He may manœuvre bodies of men by his symbols on the map and so judge of the probable result. Of course he may talk to himself during this studying over the map, but certainly the map and other physical symbols play a part in his thinking process.

So we might entertain the hypothesis that thinking is a substituting of symbolic objects and activities for the real and important ones, without limiting ourselves to implicit movements as our symbols. Or, we might entertain the hypothesis that thinking consists in implicit movements, without limiting them to speech movements. Watson means to include gesture language as well as spoken language in his hypothesis, and to include talking with the hands in the case of deaf people ; and he has no radical objection to including other implicit movements, should any appear probable ; but he pins his faith mostly to implicit movements of the speech organs.

This hypothesis strikes one as reasonable, since most of us would testify that we talked to ourselves more or less while thinking. We are often aware of our own inner speech. The reasonableness of the hypothesis rests on this common observation, which is obviously introspective. Margaret Floy Washburn, a strong supporter herself of the general motor theory of thinking, though by no means a behaviourist, has pointed out the absurdity of basing upon introspection a hypothesis designed to bolster up behaviourism.[1] We do often see lip movements and hear muttered words in another person who is thinking, but

[1] M. F. Washburn, *Psychological Review*, 1922, vol. xxix. pp. 89–112.

our own experience of inner speech is what makes the hypothesis easy to accept.

Because it thus agrees with the experience of so many of us, the hypothesis that thinking is silent speech is by no means novel, but has been advanced time and again without any reference to behaviourism. What behaviourism requires is that this inner speech must consist of actual though small movements of the speech organs. Here, to be sure, it goes beyond introspection. To some individuals, inner speech seems to be felt in the mouth and throat and respiratory organs, as if actual movements were occurring there ; while to others it seems to be auditory rather than motor. Introspection can certainly not be depended on to tell us whether or not inner speech always involves speech movements. Watson, though he allowed his hypothesis to be suggested by introspection, did not propose to test it that way. He proposed to apply delicate recording apparatus to the speech organs, in the hope of securing objective evidence of speech movements during thinking. The larynx seemed to him the most likely organ to register, with the tongue probably next.

Several investigators have endeavoured to obtain evidence for or against this hypothesis, by registering the movements of the larynx and tongue during thinking. They find movements part of the time, but not all of the time. Even in definite inner speech, when the subject recites a sentence to himself, the movements of these speech organs are slight and irregular, and betray no pattern resembling that of vocally speaking the same sentence.[1] The results to date are thus negative, but the apparatus available is still pretty crude and might fail to register very slight muscular contractions ; so that the

[1] A. M. Thorson, ' The Relation of Tongue Movements to Internal Speech,' *Journal of Experimental Psychology*, 1925, vol. viii. pp. 1–32.

hypothesis cannot be said to be disproved. It is quite possible, indeed, that the larynx is not the best place to look for implicit speech movements. The larynx, which produces ' voice,' is quiet in voiceless speech such as whispering. Now, as whispering is an intervening stage between talking aloud and silent speech, why should we expect the larynx, inactive during whispering, to spring into action again in silent speech ? The more likely place to look for movements in silent speech is the respiration ; and there is actually good evidence of prolongation and irregularity of expiration during energetic inner speech.[1] This lead has not been sufficiently followed up as yet.

Behaviourism does not stand or fall with the fortunes of this one hypothesis. Even if speech movements were always found, the question would remain what kept them going, and whether the brain action that kept them going was not closer to the heart of the process than the resulting movements. On the other hand, if speech movements should be proved certainly not to occur in all thinking, there would remain other muscular movements and tensions that might furnish the sensorimotor process required by behaviourism for every implicit activity.

While we are on this subject, I may as well tell you in a few words some reasons why I personally do not accept the equation, thought = speech. One is that I often have difficulty in finding the word required to express a meaning which I certainly have ' in mind.' I get stuck, not infrequently, for even a familiar word. Another reason is that you certainly cannot turn the equation around and say that speech = thought. You can recite a familiar passage with no sense of its meaning, and while thinking something entirely different. Finally, thinking certainly

[1] J. J. B. Morgan, ' The Overcoming of Distraction and Other Resistances,' *Archives of Psychology*, No. 35, 1916.

seems as much akin to seeing as to manipulating. It seems to consist in seeing the point, in observing relationships. Watson's speech habits substituted for actual manipulation fail to show how thinking carries you beyond your previous habits. Why should the combination of words, ' Suppose I moved the piano over there,' lead to the continuation, ' But it would jut out over the window,' just as a matter of language habit ? Something more than the words must certainly be in the game, and that something consists somehow in seeing the point.

My chief objection to behaviourism, as you may see, is that it soft-pedals so insistently on ' seeing.' Even grant, for the sake of peace, that all seeing leads to implicit motor responses, is not the seeing the important part of the sensorimotor reaction, as a preparation for overt and practical action ? Remember the subject who reports in a sensory experiment, 'I see yellow.' Is not the most important part of his whole reaction, to himself, the fact that he does see yellow ? He might have made a slip of the tongue and said yellow when he saw green, and then go ahead and make use of his observation according to what he had seen and not according to what he had said. There are a hundred forms in which this difficulty recurs.

WATSON'S VIEWS ON EMOTION AND INSTINCT

Let us turn to the theory of emotion. Watson's hypothesis is that emotion, in general, consists in ' profound changes of the bodily mechanism as a whole, but particularly of the visceral and glandular systems,' while each separate emotion is a particular pattern of such changes.[1] ' Notwithstanding the fact that in all emotional responses there are overt factors such as the movement of the eyes and the arms and the legs and the trunk, visceral

[1] *Psychology from the Standpoint of a Behaviourist*, 1919, p. 195.

and glandular factors predominate.' [1] This hypothesis obviously follows along the lines of the James-Lange theory; and indeed Watson quotes Lange with approval while pouring contempt upon James for regarding the complex of sensations resulting from the bodily changes as psychologically important, and for relying in part upon introspective evidence for his theory. To convert James into Watson, simply erase the sensations or feeling from the total emotion, leaving the bodily changes which James did so much to bring into prominence.

Though it is difficult to get at the viscera so as to test this hypothesis directly, there are some external indicators, such as pulse and blood pressure, that can be studied. There has been great activity in the past decade in studying all sorts of emotional expression, circulatory, respiratory, facial, vocal; but one disappointing result is the absence of clear patterns of emotional response or expression, to correspond to the terrifying or agreeable situations in which the subject is placed, or to his verbal report of the emotion experienced.[2] Possibly, then, two emotions cannot be distinguished simply as two visceral patterns, without taking account of the non-visceral behaviour and even of the situations in which they arise. Cannon,[3] we may remember, found a well-marked visceral pattern, consisting of hastened heart beat, constricted arteries, high blood pressure, inhibited stomach movement, all dependent on the action of the sympathetic division of the autonomic nervous system and on the secretions from the adrenal glands; but this pattern of internal processes occurred in fear, in anger, and in excited states which

[1] *Behaviourism*, 1924, p. 130.

[2] C. Landis, *Journal of Comparative Psychology*, 1924, vol. iv. pp. 447–501.

[3] W. B. Cannon, *Bodily Changes in Pain, Hunger, Fear, and Rage* (Appleton, 1929, 2nd edition).

were neither fear nor anger. The difference between fear and anger apparently lies outside the visceral sphere. It may lie in the different situations which arouse the two emotions, in the different overt reactions, or in the set or readiness for different overt reactions.

Quite apart from his special hypothesis for fitting emotion into the behaviouristic system, Watson has made important contributions to the study of emotions in children. He finds three well-marked patterns of emotional behaviour in very young infants, calling them fear, rage and love, and describing them, naturally, in terms of situation and overt response rather than in terms of implicit visceral behaviour. As he finds no others in the new-born, he regards these three as the only native emotional patterns, all others being habits formed as manual habits are, by the process of learning. The natural or original stimuli to fear were loud sounds and loss of support (slipping or falling) ; for rage, hampering of the infant's freedom of movement ; for love, patting and stroking. Experimentally, it was found possible to condition a child of eleven months by applying the sound of a steel bar struck close behind the child at the moment when he was reaching out for a white rat, to which his response was regularly positive up to this time. The loud noise called out a reflex start, and sometimes whimpering and other signs of fear or discomfort ; and by repeating the loud noise every time the child reached for the rat, the experimenter soon established a conditioned fear response to the animal. Moreover, this conditioned fear persisted. In general, it has been found difficult to extinguish conditioned fears once established. Presumably, conditioned rage and love responses can be established in the same way. The experiment thus shows how numerous irrational fears, antipathies, and affections of children may arise.[1]

[1] *Behaviourism*, 1924, p. 120.

If your acquaintance with behaviourism is derived wholly from Watson's later writings, you will accuse me of delaying till this late moment any mention of what seems to you most characteristically behaviouristic, namely, his rejection of instinct and of all hereditary mental traits, and his assertion that any normal child, with proper environment and training, can be made into ' any type of specialist I might select—doctor, lawyer, artist, merchant-chief and, yes, even beggar-man and thief, regardless of his talents, penchants, tendencies, abilities, vocations and race of his ancestors.' [1] This extreme environmentalism is not logically bound up with behaviourism. It has nothing to do with a preference for objective psychology or with disgust with introspection and consciousness. In 1914, Watson, writing mainly of animal behaviour, found a great deal to say of instinct. In 1919, while critical of the lists of human instincts given by James and Thorndike, he still recognizes a number of human instincts, and stresses the fundamental importance of instinctive activity as a basis for learning. Has Watson only gradually realized what behaviourism means ? Or have we here simply a develop-ment of his thinking on a special topic ? The behaviourist cannot be bound down for the rest of his life to the task of continually expounding the logical implications of be-haviourism. So I say, you may be a behaviourist and reject this particular view of Watson, or you may accept it though not a behaviourist. It is not a question between one school and another. It is a question of fact or of evidence, and the evidence is still coming in from investigators who work not as behaviourists or as non-behaviourists, but as students of these important and difficult questions. The question of instinct will come up again in our dis-cussion of the purposivist school. The question of the comparative importance of heredity and environment in

[1] *Behaviourism*, 1924, p. 82.

producing differences between men is one that does not fit in specially well with our plan to discuss the schools of psychology.

In one way, Watson's extreme environmentalist stand is a logical one for the behaviourist. Watson admits that his conclusion goes beyond the evidence, but he thinks it is worth while going beyond the evidence on this side of the question just because those who hold to the opposite or hereditarian view have been doing the same thing ' for many thousands of years.' This desire to shake people out of their complacent acceptance of traditional views is perhaps more characteristic of Watson's behaviourism than any of his particular views on learning, thinking, emotion, and instinct.

SOME OTHER PROMINENT BEHAVIOURISTS

In our consideration of American behaviourism, thus far, we have scarcely mentioned any one but Watson as being definitely a behaviourist. A few others should be mentioned, if only to correct the false impression that behaviourism is a one-man party.

Max Meyer of the University of Missouri, writing in 1911 on *The Fundamental Laws of Human Behaviour*,[1] came close to behaviourism, and is now regarded as a behaviourist. Born in 1873, Meyer was a pupil of the important German psychologist, Carl Stumpf of Berlin, who, like G. E. Müller, previously mentioned, was one of the younger contemporaries of Wundt who independently started psychological laboratories in the early days. Stumpf specialized in the psychology of hearing and of music, and Meyer has been a prolific contributor to this line of study, which cannot be called behaviouristic by any means. But Meyer became

[1] M. Meyer, *The Fundamental Laws of Human Behaviour* (R. G. Badger, 1911), pp. 4, 239.

much interested in the mechanism of the ear and of the brain, and came to believe that the only real science of psychology must consist of a knowledge of the laws of nerve action. What he does in this book of 1911 is to develop laws and schemes of nerve action that can account for the facts of conscious life and behaviour.

During the past few decades the conviction became general that a science of the subjective, an introspective science, because of its limited possibility of generalization, hardly deserved the name of a science. In order to remedy the defect which had been discovered, objective methods, like those used in the physical sciences, were introduced into the mental sciences, to supplement the subjective method of introspection. . . .

Not the study of the individual's consciousness of the 'structure of the mind,' but the study of the nervous laws of behaviour will enable us to understand the significance of human action for human life in the individual and in society. The scientific value of introspective psychology consists merely in the fact that it aids us in discovering the laws of nervous function.

Meyer believed, then, that introspection could be of some service to psychology, provided it was used to throw light on performance, rather than for description of experience as such.

I should like to call your attention specially to the title of another of Meyer's books, *The Psychology of the Other One*,[1] published in 1921, and used as an introductory text-book. The title at first seems odd for a general work on psychology ; you would think it dealt with some special topic. But the title embodies the author's point of view : the proper object of study in psychology is the ' other one.' He is the individual to be observed. The author thus forces the student away from the traditional conception that psychology is primarily the study of oneself. It

[1] Published by Lucas Bros.

6

should be primarily a study of other people. There are
several reasons why that is a good point of view. You are
personally concerned about your own doings, and likely to
be biased in your observation. Also, the study of other
people forces the use of objective methods.

The study of the ' other one ' does not, indeed, exclude
introspection, for you may ask that other one to serve as
your subject in an experiment, and get him to introspect
for you. Bühler, mentioned before as one of the Külpe
group who studied thought processes by introspective
methods, had made a statement that is pertinent here.
He said that the investigator in a thought experiment
should recognize that he is to study the thought processes
of other people rather than his own. The experimenter
arranges the situation, provides the stimuli, and assigns
the subject his task ; but then, as Bühler puts it, the
experimenter ceases to see with his own eyes and begins
to see with the eyes of his subject. The subject makes
the observation and reports it, but is not further concerned.
He has no concern with the hypothesis that the experimenter is testing, nor with the use made of the observation.
He simply furnishes the raw data which the experimenter
works over. If the experimenter tested his hypothesis by
observations on himself, his observation might be prejudiced. He keeps his subject as far as possible in ignorance of the purpose of the experiment, so as to secure
unprejudiced data. Such in fact was the standard procedure in laboratory work by the introspective method,
by the method of impression, and by objective methods as
well. Here as elsewhere, the practice of investigators
was in advance of the theoretical definition.

In theory and definition it was somewhat revolutionary
to conceive of psychology as the study of the other one.
Here is the psychologist, P, who says that his task is to
study experience. Well, he naturally thinks of experience

as he has it, as centring in himself. But let us suppose
that a biologist, accustomed to studying organisms, turns
psychologist, and carries over his biological point of view.
He sets himself to study an organism, O, another organism
than himself. He studies the performances of O, and he
may wish to study the experiences of O. If he can communicate with O by language, he may get O to report
experiences and may accept them as true reports of O's
experiences. The typical psychological situation thus
becomes, not P faced by the universe, but P studying an O
who is faced by the universe. This point of view was
necessarily taken by the behaviourist, but it has been taken
by introspectionists as well.

One of Meyer's pupils, A. P. Weiss of Ohio State University (born 1879) and an active experimentalist and student
of child psychology, is also to be named among the leading
behaviourists. His book, *A Theoretical Basis of Human
Behaviour* (1925),[1] sets out to show a way in which psychology can take its place among the natural sciences. He
urges psychologists to give up certain pretensions which
keep them out of the scientific fold. The particular pretension he has in mind is that psychology has access,
through introspection, to a set of realities or existences
which are not material and which are accordingly not
accessible to the physicist and chemist and biologist. He
proposes that psychology shall admit that there are no
ultimate entities besides those recognized by physics.
Physics at the present time may not have reached its
ultimate analysis, but as far as it has gone the electron and
proton seem to be the fundamental entities. Psychology,
then, says Weiss, should admit the electron and proton
as its fundamental entities and make no claim to have
another set of entities of its own. Of course, in the psychological laboratory or clinic you do not use physicists'

[1] Published by R. G. Adams & Co.

techniques and do not get very close to the electrons and protons ; but neither does the biologist nor even the chemist, who is mostly satisfied with atoms as his ultimates. But we can all take off our hats to the electrons and protons, and admit that ultimately all chemical and biological processes, including what we ordinarily know as mental processes—Weiss would certainly not use that word ' mental,' but we will do it behind his back, just to identify the processes we are talking about—we can admit that all these processes consist ultimately in the motion of electrons and protons, provided that is the ultimate physics. Psychology, then—and we agree here with Weiss—lays no claim to have a special world of its own to study, but accepts the point of view that its phenomena are natural phenomena and capable of the same ultimate analysis as all other phenomena.

Weiss proceeds to consider what you can do in psychology without assuming any entities apart from the physical entities. He finds that one of the most significant facts about the human organism is that it exists in a social environment. One individual's behaviour acts as a stimulus arousing behaviour in another individual. The individual's development is very largely controlled by the social situation in which he develops. Thus human behaviour is social. Yet it would be one-sided to stress this fact to the exclusion of the other fact that all behaviour is a biological activity. In becoming socialized, man does not become any less biological. All his processes are just as biological as if he were a solitary animal. In order to do justice to both sides, Weiss coins the word *biosocial* to characterize human behaviour. The field of psychology is that of biosocial processes, and the point of view of psychology is biosocial. It seems a good word for psychology to use, pointing as it does to the intimate contacts the psychologist should maintain with the biological sciences on one side and the social sciences on the other. Dispute sometimes arises whether psychology is to be classed with the biological or the social sciences. It is really biosocial, and its central position among the sciences that deal with man and other living creatures makes it possible for it to take a very important place in science as a whole—a position much more important than it could ever attain by pretending to have a separate world of its own to study.

While there are some differences of emphasis between the behaviourism of Weiss and that of Watson, there is no real inconsistency. Nor, on the other hand, is there any inconsistency between Weiss's conception of psychology and the use of the introspective method in the laboratory. For the subject in an experiment to report an after-image, and for the experimenter to accept that report as indicating that the subject actually saw what he reports seeing, need not imply in the least that we are examining a different world in the psychological laboratory from that observed by the physicist or biologist. The after-image is a biological process occurring in the subject's visual apparatus. Only the subject can observe it, because it is a process that only occurs as the result of suitable stimulation by light ; you, as experimenter watching the subject, cannot see that after-image simply because your own visual apparatus is not receiving the necessary stimulation. And if we can find a place for the after-image in the general world of natural processes, there is no reason why we should not find a place there for the memory-image as well, or for the toothache or any feeling of pleasantness or unpleasantness. What seems to have happened with the behaviourists is that, having been brought into contact with a philosophy that made a metaphysical puzzle of these matters, they failed to think the thing through from the standpoint of an inclusive natural science, but jumped into a violent avoiding reaction. Hearing that introspection was supposed to reveal another world, they reacted by saying, ' Away with introspection ! ' This was a reaction to a certain philosophy and not to the actual laboratory work that used the introspective method.

Another prominent behaviourist, Walter S. Hunter of Clark University (born 1889) was a pupil of Angell and also of Harvey A. Carr of the University of Chicago. (Carr, born 1873, though deserving of high mention among animal psychologists, cannot be included in a list of the behaviourists. He is a student of behaviour but not a behaviourist. There are many such.) Hunter has coined a new name for the science of human behaviour.[1] He calls it anthroponomy, literally the science of man. The word ' psychology,' he thinks, cannot properly be applied to behaviour study, for by derivation it means the study of the psychic. One might retort that words have a way of changing their meanings with the change of the times— that physics and physiology by derivation should be the same science—and that, going far enough back in the etymology of ' psychology,' we find it to mean literally the ' science of breathing.' What Hunter really desires, no doubt, is a single noun for the ' science of behaviour,' but most of us would not agree with his relinquishing the name ' psychology ' to the existentialists as their exclusive property. I will quote a few of Hunter's statements as a stimulus to your thinking, but without attempting to debate the questions suggested :

Psychology, if the word means anything, means a study of psychic factors, processes, or states. To the extent that psychology is defined as the study of immediate experience, this immediate experience is regarded as something mental. . . .

[1] See his articles in the collections, *Psychologies of 1925* (Clark University Press), and *Psychologies of 1930* (Clark University Press), and his book *Human Behaviour* (University of Chicago Press, 1928).

If we ask a contemporary psychologist what he means by the term consciousness, or experience, he will reply by enumerating such things as sweet, red, . . . roses . . . and melodies. . . . I wish to point out that consciousness or experience for the psychologist is merely a name which he applies to what other people call the environment of man. . . .

The psychologist seeks to understand human nature by calling the external and internal environments mental and then by proceeding to the study and analysis of these environments. . . . The psychological method of studying man is thus an indirect one in the sense that the conclusions concerning human nature are drawn from an ostensible study of human environments. Such a method was theoretically worthy of a trial fifty years ago. Its failure as a method for the analysing of human nature gave rise to anthroponomy.

The general method of anthroponomy is a method of direct observation and experiment using organic human behaviour as its subject-matter. . . . The aspects of human behaviour which are most peculiarly the concern of anthroponomy are language behaviour, learning, inter-stimulation and response, and the prediction of behaviour on the basis of sample performances. . . . Anthroponomy also interests itself in many other phases of human behaviour. It studies the genetic aspects of human behaviour through the medium of animal and child behaviour. And it is seriously concerned with abnormal behaviour and with sense-organ function.

Besides his contributions to the theoretical basis of behaviourism, Hunter is well known for important contributions to the science itself—whatever it be named—especially for his discovery of the ' delayed reaction ' in animals and children.

BEHAVIOUR AND THE BRAIN, AS STUDIED BY FRANZ AND LASHLEY

Without extending our roster of active behaviourists to too great a length, we certainly must not omit Lashley, one of the most productive of all. Born in 1890, Lashley was a psychological, or behaviouristic son of Watson, though always a man of independent judgement. Here are some quotations indicative of his behaviouristic trend.[1] He announces himself as opposed to subjectivism, and to any pretension of introspection to reveal a unique mode of existence not definable in objective terms. 'The subjectivist claims a universe of non-material things as the subject of his study'—this subjectivist, by the way, cannot be the existential psychologist, who starts by saying that the raw data of physics and psychology are the same. 'The behaviourist denies sensations, images, and all other phenomena which the subjectivist claims to find by introspection.' This is the regular behaviouristic stand. But Lashley goes on to show that all the findings of introspection that are genuine can be expressed in objective terms, and so find a place in a behaviouristic psychology. Without assuming to evaluate his performance of this task, to judge whether he did justice to all the genuine findings of introspection, or to decide whether he fully succeeded in translating them all into objective terms, we can recognize that his conclusion is interesting in two ways. It would show that subjectivism was entirely unnecessary in psychology ; but it would also show that behaviourism, after all, had no fundamental objection to introspection. Behaviourists might be critical of it and cautious in their use of it, because of its undoubted difficulties and pitfalls as a method of observation ; but their objection could not be fundamental if they can translate the results of introspection into objective terms and adopt them into their psychology.

What Lashley, Watson, and the other behaviourists mean when they deny sensations and images is more, I admit, than I have ever been able to make out. Take

[1] K. S. Lashley, ' The Behaviouristic Interpretation of Consciousness,' *Psychological Review*, 1923, vol. xxx, pp. 237–72, 329–53.

images. What do they do with a person who says, ' When I read what you have written, I can just hear the tone of your voice,' or with one who says, ' When I hear your voice over the telephone, I can see your face,' or with one who reports a dream in which he saw and heard certain things ? Do they mean that these people are simply lying, or that they are following a tradition which amounts to an unfounded superstition ? Apparently they are not quite so disdainful as that, but rather mean that the image is not what it is taken to be, is not visual or auditory (except in so far as actually present visual or auditory stimuli may play a part in it), but really some sort of implicit motor activity, such as inner speech. Such a view would be a respectable hypothesis to explain the image, but it would grant the reality of the image—otherwise there would be nothing to explain. In the same way, Watson's hypothesis that thinking is subvocal speech is worthy of consideration, but does not in the least do away with the fact of thinking.

Exactly where the bogy of subjectivism hides himself nowadays I cannot guess. It seems to me I have not seen him rear his head in psychological circles for lo ! these thirty years or more. But he must be somewhere about, for do we not see the behaviourists charging all over the field and jousting at him ?

But it would not be fair to Lashley to leave the impression that he has been mostly engaged in jousting. He has done much work and made many valuable contributions to animal and physiological psychology. Best known is his work on the localization of the higher functions in the cortex of the brain. His negative findings have compelled the attention of physiologists as well as of psychologists.

The story of brain localization starts with Gall, the phrenologist, about 1800. Gall, an anatomist of scientific spirit, was impressed by the queer-shaped heads of certain individuals whose mental traits were also peculiar, and conceived the idea that unequal development of various parts of the brain was responsible both for the peculiar traits and for the shape of the skull. He believed it possible to map out the surface of the brain into a large number of areas, one for friendliness, one for acquisitiveness, one for reverence, one for wit, one for language, one for number, and so on. This phrenological system of localization was not based on any direct physiological study of the brain. When, about 1825, physiologists began experimenting on the brains of animals, they could find nothing approaching Gall's scheme of localized organs, and Flourens, the leading brain physiologist of the time, announced that the brain functioned as a whole. About 1870, more exact work enabled physiologists to begin marking out certain areas which were definitely connected with certain functions, but these functions had no resemblance to Gall's list. Before 1900, there was definite proof by a combination of anatomical and physiological methods with the study of brain injuries in man, that each of the major senses had a circumscribed area of the cortex. The retina of the eye, for example, is connected by nerve fibres with a relatively small area in the occipital lobe, at the rear of the brain, and complete destruction of this area, in man, renders the individual blind. Besides the sensory areas, the motor area was localized. It has the most direct connexions with the muscles, anatomically, and its destruction in man brings motor paralysis. The World War, with its numerous bullet and shrapnel wounds affecting small circumscribed spots of the cortex, gave abundant opportunity for testing these conclusions, and they were amply confirmed.

But all the sensory and motor areas together make up but a small part of the cortex of man. In microscopic structure, the rest of the cortex is by no means uniform, and on the probable assumption that difference of structure means difference of function, it was believed that further localizations, localizations of higher functions, should be possible.

If the higher functions were to be studied in reference to their localization, it was time for psychologists to unite with the physiologists in the study. Franz, who united both sciences in his own person, undertook this task. Franz (born 1874) was a pupil of Cattell and for several years his chief assistant in the Columbia laboratory, where for one of these years Thorndike was engaged in his studies of animal learning. Franz next devoted several years to physiology, and shortly after 1900 he devised a method of studying the localization of higher functions by combining the Thorndike methods of training and testing animals with the physiological method of extirpating portions of the brain. To see, for example, whether the frontal lobes of a cat were concerned in the learned reaction of escaping from a cage by turning a button he first had the animal learn the trick, then removed the frontal lobes, allowed the animal time to recover from the shock of the operation, and then tested the animal to see if the trick were retained. If not, he proceeded to give the animal the opportunity to learn the trick again. His results on the frontal lobes showed that loss of this part of the brain brought a loss of tricks that had been learned, but did not prevent the animal from relearning the same tricks with about the same facility as before the injury. Franz followed this fruitful lead for many years with valuable results, including some of practical value on the re-education of human paralysed and aphasic patients.[1]

[1] S. I. Franz, *American Journal of Physiology*, 1902, vol. viii. pp. 1–22 ; *Archives of Psychology*, No. 2, 1907 ; and many later papers.

Lashley started on this line of study as a collaborator with Franz. In 1917 they showed the results of applying the combined training and extirpation method to that favourite laboratory animal, the white rat, a very convenient animal for learning experiments, though, to be sure, further removed from man in brain development than the cat or monkey. Lashley has followed this line of study assiduously and with striking though somewhat baffling results. Certainly his results, like those of Franz, baffle any one who expects to find a small sharply localized centre for each learned performance. While loss of any considerable amount of the cortex slows up the rat's learning, it seems to make little difference to the rat what part of the cortex is removed and what part is left for him to learn with. He apparently learns the maze as well with one part as with another. The greater the amount of cortex removed, the more he is hampered in his learning. Easy tricks, indeed, are learned fairly quickly even with only a half of the cortext left, but difficult tricks are almost impossible to learn with so little cortex left. Lashley summarizes his findings under two principles.[1]

The principle of equipotentiality : any part of the cortex is potentially the same as any other in its ability to take part in any sort of learned performance. The sensory and motor areas are not included in this statement.

The principle of mass action : the cortext acts as a whole, so that the more cortex there is available, the more effectively it operates and the more quickly the animal learns.

The study of cortical function is bound to be intricate and difficult, and we cannot hope that Lashley has said the final word on it. That the ' cortex functions as a whole ' cannot be taken literally, but rather in the sense that it functions in wide-spreading patterns or dynamic systems,

[1] K. S. Lashley, *Brain Mechanisms and Intelligence* (University of Chicago Press, 1929), p. 25.

and not in sharply localized centres. As Lashley points out, the whole tendency of his results is against accepting the simple reflex arc as the unit out of which brain function is built up. Hence we cannot, by superimposing the idea of the conditioned reflex upon that of the simple reflex, believe that we have furnished the key to all learned behaviour. Another result of Lashley, following up work of Watson, serves to reinforce this conclusion. Running through a maze can be thought of as a series of steps and turns, and was easily thought of as a chain of reflexes. Watson showed that rats which had learned a maze could still run it perfectly though deprived, by operation, of sight, smell, hearing, or most of touch, and even though deprived of all of these senses. He concluded that the remaining sense, that is the muscle sense, must furnish the sensory cues that enabled the animal to follow the learned path, and accordingly interpreted the running of a maze as a chain of reflexes, each movement providing through the muscle sense the stimulus for the next in order. But Lashley found a way of removing the muscle sense also, by cutting its conduction path in the spinal cord—and still the rats ran the maze perfectly. He also found evidence that a rat, in learning a maze, obtained a sort of general orientation or steer in the direction of the exit, so that his maze running was not a simple chain of reflexes. No doubt these recent findings of Lashley have been somewhat disturbing to many behaviourists, who liked the reflex, the conditioned reflex, and the reflex chain, because they seemed to furnish a simple interpretation of behaviour and to banish ' mystery.' Yet I do not understand that behaviourism is tied to any one hypothesis or explanation in such a way as to be seriously shaken when that particular explanation has to make way for one more adequate ; for behaviourism is a spirit or attitude rather than any fixed theory.

An interesting aspect of these recent discoveries is that they bring the behaviourists and the Gestalt psychologists —of whom we have to treat in the next chapter—closer together than at one time seemed possible.

THE SIGNIFICANCE OF BEHAVIOURISM

I am prepared to believe that the historian fifty years hence, looking back on these first thirty years of the century, will assign much significance to the movement which we now call behaviourism ; but I admit that I am puzzled to guess exactly where he will find its significance to lie. It has made a strong appeal to the younger generation of psychologists and to some who are not so young ; and it has made an even stronger appeal outside of the ranks of the psychologists. Just what is the nature of its appeal, and what are its elements of vitality ?

Behaviourism first appeared as a reform in methodology. It urged the use of objective methods and decried the use of introspection. We cannot assign it the credit of introducing the objective method into psychology, for that method had long been used. It did not introduce the animal experiment into psychology, unless, indeed, we follow the European psychologists who, looking at our American doings from a little distance, count in Thorndike as the arch behaviourist. To do that would be to date behaviourism from 1898 instead of from 1912, to minimize the debate over the ' law of effect,' and to widen the behaviouristic group considerably. Possibly that is what the historian fifty years hence will do with us. If so, he will probably also include Pavlov and Bechterev and so be able to credit behaviourism with the invention of the conditioned reflex method of experimentation. Apart from that, he might find it difficult to credit behaviourism with the invention of any particular objective method.

We cannot assign to behaviourism the credit of having forced the elimination of introspection from psychology, for the introspective psychologists have continued their work, some of it very important work, and there is no indication that introspection is going to be eliminated. We have seen the behaviourists admitting it under the name of ' verbal report,' and showing that its findings can be taken over into an objective psychology. We have seen that the use of introspection as a method of investigation does not commit the investigator to any subjectivism, and that it is consistent with a thoroughly ' natural science ' conception of psychology.

Behaviourism has had more influence on the terms and concepts employed by psychologists than upon their methods of obtaining their data. Formerly, psychologists who were really studying performance were apt to adopt the convention of saying they were studying some ' modification of consciousness,' an expression which was as absurd from the point of view of the existentialist as from any other, since he was perfectly clear himself on the difference between describing performance and describing experience as such. A large share of psychological work consists in the study of performance, and behaviourists have done a service to psychology by forcing us to speak in terms of performance when that is what we mean.

But we cannot suppose that people outside the ranks of psychology would allow themselves to become excited over the psychologist's technical problems of terms, concepts, and methods. Why should the general public be disturbed to learn that introspection was practised in certain psychological laboratories, or that certain psychologists pretended to be conscious and to have sensations, images, feelings, and desires, and why should the public acclaim the bold knight who set forth to eradicate these superstitions ? That section of the public which became involved in college courses in psychology would to be sure welcome the simplifications which behaviourism seemed to introduce. Some of the simplifications were purely verbal, and some of the ' mysteries ' eliminated with a wave of the hand remained in the form of unsolved problems ; but other simplifications were genuine, for behaviourism certainly helped in their road to oblivion some unpsychological problems inherited from philosophy.

But the significance of behaviourism transcends the limits of psychology. It extends into sociology. Here I have an advertisement of a ' new kind of sociology text,' which is stated to be ' consistently and frankly behaviouristic. The authors keep their eyes on concrete problems in American life and discuss them on the basis of verifiable material.' Now if our behaviourism has really enabled the sociologists to tackle concrete problems after the manner of natural science, then behaviourism has indeed great significance.

But the significance of behaviourism must go beyond even that. Here I have some notices of Watson's book entitled *Behaviourism,* which is certainly not one of his most scientific books from the psychologist's point of view. But it did make great claims. Here is what the *Nation* of London says of it :

His new book claims to put forward not only a new methodology, not even merely a body of psychological theory, but a system which will, in his opinion, revolutionize ethics, religion, psycho-analysis—in fact, all the mental and moral sciences.

If we turn back to the book, with this notice in mind, we find Watson saying that behaviourism is the natural science that takes as its field all of human behaviour and adjustments, which it studies by experimental methods, with the object of controlling man's behaviour in accordance with the findings of science. He says that the growing success of this natural science approach to human problems is causing philosophy to disappear and become the history of science, that it envisages the development of an experimental ethics to take the place of the old authoritative and speculative ethics, based on religion, and that it will gradually do away with psycho-analysis and replace it by scientific studies of the child's development and by such control of that development as will prevent the psychopathic breakdowns which now have to be treated in adult life. He states his system in about as many words as I have used in my paraphrase. It is a programme rather than a system, and a hope rather than a programme.

But it was significant that a man who had won the public ear as a representative of science should give vigorous expression to this hope. The New York *Times* said of the book, ' It marks an epoch in the intellectual history of man.'

That is doing pretty well for the *Times*. Now let us hear the *Tribune* : ' Perhaps this is the most important book ever written. One stands for an instant blinded with a great hope.'

The reference here may be to what seems the most striking of Watson's assertions in that book, the assertion that he could take any healthy, well-formed child, and make of him anything you chose, provided he had full control of that child's environment. This also was only a programme, as he admitted a little later in the book, saying that the bold statement was meant as a challenge, and that his real motive was to induce the public to provide for the very extensive research required on the development of the child. He was right there ; we do need such research, and it might have the results which he predicts. But at the present time, if you delivered into his care a number of healthy babies with instructions that he should make of each a great artist, or a great business man, or a great public leader, I am sure he would be utterly puzzled

7

as to how to proceed. Neither he nor any one else possesses at present the requisite scientific knowledge. But at any rate that may have been the hope that blinded the reviewer.

It is the moral qualities of the behaviouristic movement, rather than its scientific achievements, that give it its present public significance. It is its boldness, freedom, tough-mindedness, and unlimited faith in the ability of science to take charge of human affairs. As one of my students, representing the generation that has grown up since the War, has said to me, behaviourism means for many a new hope and a new orientation when the old guide-posts have become hopelessly discredited. It is a religion to take the place of religion.

CHAPTER IV

GESTALT PSYCHOLOGY OR CONFIGURATIONISM

JUST when behaviourism was emerging in America a small group of young psychologists in Germany started on a line of thought that revolutionized their conceptions of the aim and method of psychology, and that gave rise to one of the most vigorous of the present-day schools. Though of the same age as behaviourism, this school has only gradually become known in the United States, and appears to us as the youngest of the schools.

This group used the word ' Gestalt ' as its slogan, and is called the Gestalt school. ' Gestalt ' is a common German word, meaning ' shape ' or ' form.' Often ' pattern ' conveys the idea. For psychological use, ' configuration ' has been suggested as an English equivalent, and the Gestalt psychologists are sometimes called the ' configurationists.'

THE RADICALISM OF GESTALT PSYCHOLOGY

The first thing to understand with regard to this new school is that, like the others, it began as a revolt against the established order. It broke with the orthodox psychology of its time. It rebelled specifically against Wundt, and more generally against associationism, that system of psychology which had come down from the seventeenth and eighteenth centuries and which largely, though by no means completely, dominated psychological theory in the nineteenth century.

Associationism had two characteristics : it aimed at analysis, and it was mostly concerned with the intellectual side of life. It had come to think of itself as a sort of mental chemistry, seeking elementary processes or experiences and their laws of combination. Fixing its attention mostly on the intellectual side of life, it sought for the simplest processes of knowing, or for the simplest experiences that give any knowledge, and accepted simple sensations as the elementary processes out of which complex experiences and ideas are built up.

Behaviourism and Gestalt psychology both revolted against this same established view of psychology, but they revolted very differently. Behaviourism revolted against the intellectualistic bias of the older psychology, and insisted that an animal or man must be taken as a moving or behaving organism. Gestalt psychology revolted against analysis as the fundamental problem of psychology. Where behaviourism had said, ' We must analyse behaviour, not experience,' the Gestalt psychologists said, ' We shall never get far in psychology by analysis of either behaviour or experience.' Behaviourism rejected the old phrase, ' association of ideas,' in favour of ' association of stimulus and motor response ' ; while Gestalt psychology believed that the whole notion of association was misleading. Both rejected sensations, at least elementary sensations, but for different reasons : behaviourism because a sensation was not a motor response, and Gestalt psychology because it was supposed to be an element or atom of experience. Behaviourism favoured the reflex as the psychological element, and liked the idea of conditioned or associated reflexes as showing how complex behaviour was built up out of the elementary reflexes. Gestalt psychology was as opposed to the simple reflex as to the simple sensation. Behaviourism disliked introspection because it purported to reveal experience instead of behaviour, while the Gestalt psychology had no objection to introspection in a broad sense, but did object seriously to the analytical type of introspection which was put forward by the existentialists as the only genuine method of obtaining psychological data. Existentialism appeared to the behaviourists as tainted with subjectivism and almost with supernaturalism, and to the Gestalt psychologists as artificial.

To show you the system against which the Gestalt psychologists specially revolted, let me refer you to Wundt's way of outlining the task of psychology. He starts by saying that experience comes in complexes or compounds, not in elements. Every experience, every idea, every emotion, every intention to act, is complex. Therefore, the job of psychology is first to analyse these complex processes into their elements, and then to study how the elements are combined and the laws of their combination. First identify the elements, and then work up to larger and larger compounds. The Gestalt psychologists called this a brick and mortar psychology, with emphasis on the brick, because the trouble was to find the mortar. The mortar problem had been a serious one for the associationists. Some of them had seen no problem, and others had appeared satisfied with the mere word, ' associations,' as an answer to the question, ' What holds the elements together ? ' Opponents of associationism had pointed to its bankruptcy in this regard, and had argued for accepting a mind or soul or ego as the agent that did the combining. James had shown that the difficulty arose from assuming the elements or atoms, which are not given in experience since experience admittedly comes in complex formations. If the elements are unreal, artificial, we need nothing real to hold them together. James argued, then, that the whole analytic-synthetic problem in psychology was a manufactured and not a real problem.

This echo from the past will serve to show that the Gestalt psychology had some historical background. More important than the argumentative discussion of this old problem of the whole and the parts, or of the 'many and the one,' was the introduction into psychology of the notion of form quality, or pattern quality—in German, ' Gestalt-qualität.' A study on that subject by von Ehrenfels in 1890 had made quite an impression in psychology. A form quality is a property possessed by a whole which is not possessed by any of the parts making up the whole. A melody, for example, is made up of the notes of the scale, but is not present in these notes taken singly but only when they are arranged in a certain sequence or pattern. Many melodies can be formed from the same notes. Put the notes together in one way, and a certain tune emerges ; put the same notes together in another way and you have an altogether different tune. More than that—you can change to a different key, thus taking a new set of notes to work with, and by arranging this second set of notes suitably, you get the same tune as in the first key. In musical language, you can transpose a tune from one key to another, so changing all the notes or ' elements,' but not changing the tune. When you recognize a tune, it is not the notes that you recognize, but the tune itself. The melody, then, has a form quality of its own. There are many other examples. A pattern of dots has a shape or design which is not to be found in the dots, and which will remain the same though the dots are changed in colour. Different forms, figures, or patterns can be made out of the same elements, and the same pattern out of different elements. The properties of wholes evidently deserved psychological study as well as the properties of elements.

From 1890 on, psychologists had seen that there was

some difficulty in fitting the form qualities into the scheme of psychology. Efforts were made to find a place for them among the elements, just as some of the imageless thought psychologists had been led to speak of thought elements. But the Gestalt school, beginning in 1912, urged that the whole distinction of elements and compounds was misleading in psychology. They further urged that the properties of organized wholes furnished the problem most worth while in psychology. We should forget that old problem of elements, and study organized wholes as they occur in experience and in performance. Under what conditions does a certain pattern occur? That is the real question, they held—a question that needs to be asked over and over again in every chapter and problem in psychology.

GESTALT PSYCHOLOGY STRESSES ORGANIZED WHOLES

If the Gestalt psychologists had contented themselves with theoretical considerations such as have just been reviewed, their school would not have shown the great vitality that it does show. They were experimentalists, however, and proceeded to take their guiding principle into the laboratory and to follow its lead in devising many novel and suggestive experiments. They have studied problems new and old—mostly old, but approached from a new angle; and they have obtained results which challenge the attention of all psychologists.

Perhaps I can give you a preliminary notion of their type of approach by citing their attack upon a problem which is very concrete though not so fundamental. That is the matter of facial expression of emotion and of character. Other psychologists have unhesitatingly gravitated toward an analytical study of this problem. They have taken each feature separately and considered the different positions it takes, seeking to discover what is expressed by each. Brow elevated, brow depressed, eyes wide, eyes half closed, lips protruded, lips retracted—each such detail probably means some relatively simple emotional state, and adding them together we get the expression of a complex emotional state.[1]

The Gestalt psychologist approaches this matter with the idea that the face must be taken as a whole. Of course, to get any results, he has to consider something besides the mere totality of the face ; he has to consider parts in a way ; but he considers them in relation to the total.[2] He finds that the apparent expression of a part may change, in a picture, when the rest of the face is changed without any objective change in that particular part. Or, if the upper part of the face, including the eyes, is first shown, and then the rest of the face is uncovered also, the eyes themselves seem to change their expression.[3] Working with silhouettes, he found that even a slight alteration of one part of the profile might seem to change the line of the whole face and give a different character to the whole ; while other changes might be considerable in themselves but make little difference to the whole expression. The same chin, introduced into two profiles otherwise quite different, would even seem different in shape as well as in expression. Evidently the shape of the face resides in the face as a whole, and the expression of the face likewise.

In the same vein, the Gestalt psychologist urges that we get no true picture of a person's character by listing the

[1] E. G. Boring and E. B. Titchener, *American Journal of Psychology*, 1923, vol. xxxiv. pp. 471–85.

[2] R. Arnheim, *Psychologische Forschung*, 1928, vol. xi. pp. 1–132.

[3] It should be noted that this same fact had been discovered by a psychologist who was not an adherent of the Gestalt School. K. Dunlap, *Genetic Psychology Monographs* (Clark University Press, 1927), vol. ii. pp. 197–233.

various personality traits, giving the individual a rating or measurement in each trait, and finally placing his ratings side by side in a table or diagram. Such a table fails to show which trait is central and dominating in the individual's personality, and which traits are of secondary importance in his case. It does not show the rôle or function of each single trait in the total personality. The personality is not a mere sum of traits, but an organized whole, a gestalt.

A mere sum, or pure sum, is one in which each item is independent of the others and simply counts for one in making up the sum. In arithmetic we have pure sums, but they are abstract. In the concrete it is not so easy to be sure that an aggregate really consists of independent items. The sum of all the dining-room tables in an apartment house is a pure sum to all intents and purposes. If you describe each of them separately and write down the descriptions in a list, you have gone as far as is necessary. You need not go on to consider how the aggregate of those tables affects the characteristics of each one. But it is easier, even in inorganic nature, to find examples of organized wholes than of wholes that are pure sums of their parts. The solar system, for example, is an organized whole, a physical gestalt, since the motion of every body in it is influenced by the presence of every other one. Let me give you one or two further examples of a physical gestalt.

A rolling wheel is an example, because the motion of each part depends on the form of the whole. To make the matter clearer, let us construct a wooden wheel, of a sort, by inserting in the hub a dozen rods for spokes, and sticking on the outer end of each rod a wooden ball, so that the rim of the wheel is made up of the dozen balls. Such a wheel would roll, though jerkily. Now as we certainly built the wheel out of hub, spokes, and balls, we might think it logical to say that the motion of the whole was composed of the motion of each of these parts. But when we observe the motion of one of the balls, we find it to describe a series of up-and-down scallops, or cycloid curves, being forced into this peculiar motion by its attachment to the wheel and by the circular shape of the whole wheel. Each ball does not roll or bounce away as an independent unit.

A soap bubble is a good example ; for if you break one little part the whole structure collapses. Electricity furnishes many examples, since the dynamo, the branching wires, and all the lights or motors in the circuit are interdependent, and a change anywhere in the circuit changes the current at every point.

The human or animal organism is certainly a gestalt. It is an organized whole, and not a mere sum of parts and organs. Through the circulation, and through the nervous system, all parts of the organism are interrelated. Some parts, to be sure, are more closely interconnected than others, so that the organism behaves as a complex unit rather than as a simple unit. But every one would probably agree in principle to the proposition that the organism acts as a whole. Its behaviour does not consist of a mere sum of reflexes. Sherrington, one of the greatest investigators of reflexes, said that the simple reflex was a convenient abstraction, and devoted his efforts largely to demonstrating the ' integrative action of the nervous system.' Pavlov studied the dependence of one conditioned reflex upon another. Watson insists that we think with our whole body, though the speech organs may play the leading rôle. Lashley is led to the conclusion that the brain functions as a whole. And I should mention here the recent studies of Coghill [1] on the development of behaviour in tadpoles. He has carefully observed both

[1] G. E. Coghill, *Anatomy and the Problems of Behaviour* (The Macmillan Co., 1929).

the earliest reactions of these young creatures and the development of their nervous systems. The earliest response which they make consists of a bending of the body away from a stimulus—a simple avoiding reaction. As the nervous system develops, this bending becomes double and passes over into the wriggling movement of swimming. The animal never passes through a stage of unco-ordinated separate movements, which it later combines into larger acts, but from the start its movements are integrated movements of the whole organism. The development is from a simple movement of the whole organism to a more elaborate movement of the whole organism.

So we find many students of behaviour in agreement on this matter. But there is no doubt that the Gestalt psychologists have insisted most strongly on the organized wholeness of behaviour, and have made the most use of this idea as a guiding principle in research.

GESTALT STUDIES OF SENSE PERCEPTION

It is high time I introduced to you some of the psychologists composing this group, for though it is an organized whole, it is really made up of individuals. The three original leaders were Max Wertheimer, Kurt Koffka, and Wolfgang Köhler. In 1912, these young psychologists were working together at the Academy, now the University, of Frankfurt. Wertheimer (born 1880) was the oldest and seems to have been the leading spirit at the start. He had already done a well-known piece of work on the use of the free association test for the detection of hidden knowledge—the detective use of this test, sometimes used in examining persons suspected of a crime. Koffka (born 1886) had done important work on imagery and thought. Köhler (born 1887), a pupil of Stumpf of Berlin, had specialized effectively in problems of tone and hearing. Köhler and Wertheimer are now at the University of Berlin, which has become the great centre for Gestalt psychology, while Koffka is now in America, as research professor at Smith College. Quite a number of younger German psychologists are definite adherents of the school, and there are several adherents in America, of whom I will mention R. M. Ogden and R. H. Wheeler.

In Frankfurt in 1912, then, Wertheimer was conducting some experiments on the seeing of motion, and Koffka and Köhler were serving as his subjects. The problem might be called one in the psychology of motion pictures. It may not be known to you that motion pictures originated about one hundred years ago, and that they were invented by a psychologist, or at least by a physiologist who was one of the forerunners of experimental psychology. Plateau, a Belgian physiologist, invented a little device for presenting a series of drawings in rapid succession, each one being seen just in a momentary flash ; but if the drawings represented an animal in successive stages of a movement, the observer, seeing a rapid succession of these still pictures, got an impression of the animal in motion. What has happened since in the technique of motion pictures is the invention of photography and the development of the motion picture camera and projector. But the rudiments of the matter remain as in Plateau's time. The motion picture camera takes a series of snapshots, each of which, taken alone, is a still view. The projector is so arranged as to show these snapshots as a series of still views, with no motion of the picture on the screen. The projector cuts off the light while the film is moving from one view to the next, for if the picture were allowed actually to move on the screen, the audience would see a blur and not the motion of the objects photographed. If you saw what is physically presented on the screen, you would see a series of still views separated by brief intervals of darkness. You cannot see what is physically presented, however. First, you cannot see the intervals of darkness because the visual sensation outlasts the physical stimulus and holds over till the next exposure, provided the interval is not too long. If it is too long, you get some flicker. But, second, you cannot see the series of still views because, somehow or other, your brain responds to that kind of a stimulus by seeing motion through the series of positions and not the separate positions themselves. You know that in watching a person actually walking or running, you do not and cannot see the successive positions that he goes through ; for if you take a snapshot of him during his motion, you often find the picture to show what looks like a very odd position. You can scarcely believe that he assumed that position in the course of his movement ; and yet the camera did not lie. If you placed this snapshot in a series of successive views, and projected the series on the screen, the person's movement would appear perfectly natural. The fact is, then, that you cannot pick out the successive positions either from a continuous motion or from a series of still views presenting those positions in rapid succession. You are forced by your organization to see the motion as a continuous whole and not as a sum of the successive positions.

Here, then, we have a very real and important problem in the dynamics of brain activity. And it is no solution to point to the succession of still views as the parts or elements of the total experience of seeing motion ; for these elements do not contain the motion that demands explanation.

Wertheimer, in working over this problem,[1] was convinced that the attempt to proceed by analysis of the total experience of seeing motion into elements, such as the

[1] M. Wertheimer, *Zeitschrift für Psychologie*, 1912, vol. lxi. pp 161–265.

successive positions, was going to lead nowhere. It seemed to him that the line of advance was to study the conditions under which motion appeared or did not appear. He simplified the ' pictures ' to the limit, simply showing first a vertical line and then a similar line a little farther to the right or left. Just two lines, one after the other, with a blank interval between. He varied the length of the blank interval. If it were as long as a second, the observer simply saw one still line and then the other still line, precisely according to the physical fact. He proceeded to decrease the blank interval between the exposures of the two lines. He cut it down to a fifth of a second, and still the observer saw first one still line and then the other. He cut the interval down still more, and the observer began to see an appearance of motion across from the first line to the second. When he reduced the interval to $1/15$ or 0.060 of a second, the observer saw a clear motion from the first position to the second. A single line seemed to move across. When the interval was further diminished, the motion became less clear, and at an interval of $1/30$ or 0.030 second, no apparent motion remained, but the two lines appeared to stand still side by side.

Wertheimer varied the experiment in several ways. If he exposed a horizontal followed by a vertical line, at the proper interval there was the appearance of a line swinging around through ninety degrees. By suitable presentations, he could get two lines appearing to move in opposite directions at the same time—a result which was important because it ruled out the eye movement explanation. The eyes could not simultaneously follow two movements in opposite directions. Wertheimer proposed an explanation which, in general terms, supposed the brain action in responding to the two successive stimuli to consist in a continuous change. That is to say, the brain did not first get one position, then the second position, each for itself, and then proceed to synthesize them into a perception of motion ; but, when the two positions came at a suitable interval, the response to the first position merged by a gradual shift into the response to the second position. Motion was not inferred but actually sensed, because the primary reception process of the brain was a moving or shifting process.

If we mean by sensation all the primary response of the brain to stimulation of the sense organs, we see that the motion is included in the sensation, according to Wertheimer's view. The Gestalt psychologists have gone on to the view that much of our experience which had been regarded as built upon sensation by higher mental processes is really included in sensation. Consider the apparent size of seen objects. If a man moves away from you from a distance of ten feet to a distance of twenty feet, his optical image upon the retina diminishes to half its first dimensions, yet he looks about as large as before. The usual explanation has been that we have *learned to interpret* the size of the retinal image in relation to the distance of the object, so that the apparent constancy of size of the same object at different distances from the eye is not a matter of sensation but of higher, learned interpretation. The Gestalt psychologists doubt this. They urge that the sensory brain process is part and parcel of the total situation, and thus subjected to the influence of the distance of the object, and that in this total situation the primary brain response gives the constancy of size. There are many similar cases in which we seem to ourselves, naïvely, to see things as they objectively are, but in which the physiology of the eye shows that we cannot really *see* them as they are, if our seeing corresponds precisely to the stimulation received by the eye. Consequently, psychologists have been accustomed to say that we do not really see those facts, but infer them, or reach them by a process of association based on past experience. In all such cases, the Gestalt psychologists hope to show that seeing, in the sense of the primary brain response to the situation, does give the facts directly. They hold, then, that the primary brain response does not depend simply on the stimulation received by the retina, but also on other factors in the total situation. Any stimulation reaching the brain is taken up into a dynamic interacting system, and its effect there depends on the total activity going on in the brain.

The associationists had thought of each little item of stimulation coming in from the sense organs as an independent unit, and of all the units as aggregating into the total brain activity of that particular moment. These items were the ultimate parts or elements of the total process, and by their summation determined the total process. The Gestalt psychologists hold that the total process controls the brain response to the separate items of stimulation.

We may see more clearly in this matter if we bring in the question of how much is native and how much learned in the perception of objects. Associationism had rejected ' innate ideas ' and all native knowledge of objects. By nature, it held, the sense organs furnish only raw data, and all knowledge or use of the data must be acquired by experience and learning. The raw data from the eye, for example, consists of a mosaic of points of light, shade and colour—a field that may be either uniform or variegated, but is wholly unorganized. What we seem to see, indeed, consists of shapes and objects in space, but that, psychologists have usually told us, is because we have learned to interpret the manifold of coloured spots. We have learned to know objects by handling them while seeing them, and have associated the visual appearance of the object with what our hands tell us of it. We have seen many circular objects, and have come to recognize certain aggregates of visual spots as indicating a circle. If we could for a moment lay aside all that we had learned and see the field of view just as the eyes present it, we should see a mere mosaic of variegated spots, free of meaning, of objects, of shapes and patterns. Such is the traditional associationist view of the matter.

To understand the Gestalt point of view, we need to make a distinction. Organization of the visual field does two different things for us. It gives us visual shapes or figures, without regard to their significance as objects. And it gives us known objects, trees, clouds, persons. Now when we know an object, we know something more than its visual shape and appearance. We know more than the eyes directly show us. The tree, with the shade under it, looks cool, i.e. suggests how it will feel to the skin to lie down under that tree. Undoubtedly, we have had to *learn* that the visual appearance means a cool spot ; and in the same way we have had to acquire all the objective meanings of the visual patterns that we see. But it is quite another question whether we have had to learn to see the shapes and patterns themselves. Undoubtedly, again, we learn to know these shapes with more precision by studying over them. But the question remains whether we had to learn to see the shapes as compact masses of colour standing out against their background. The pure associationist doctrine says we had to learn even that ; the Gestalt psychology thinks not.

Suppose as we open our eyes on a certain occasion we have nothing before us but a green blotch on a grey background. We unhesitatingly take the blotch as a coherent whole, as a vague shape standing out from its background. We can scarcely force ourselves to take half of the green blotch along with a part of the adjacent grey as a unit, still less to take part of the green blotch along with distant parts of the grey, and see that combination as a unit.

8

But the association doctrine, taken strictly, would teach that there is nothing in the natural seeing process to lead us to take compact blotches as units in preference to any other combination of points from various parts of the field. We have learned to see compact forms as units, because compact visual forms so often mean objects of practical importance. If we have had to learn this lesson, we have certainly learned it well, for it is well-nigh impossible to see a novel and meaningless field in any other way. So there is prima facie evidence for the Gestalt contention, which is that we do not have to learn to see a compact blotch as a unit, because the primary brain response to the area of homogeneous stimulation is a dynamic system and not an aggregation of separately active points.[1]

FIGURE AND GROUND IN GESTALT PSYCHOLOGY

This distinction of figure and ground is regarded by the Gestalt psychologists as absolutely fundamental in the process of seeing. Some figure is sure to be seen if the field offers any possibility of it. The figure is typically compact, but at any rate it appears as having form and outline, while the background appears like unlimited space. The figure is more apt to attract attention than the ground. When the baby first opens his eyes upon the world, while he certainly does not see a world of objects such as adults know and see, he may not, on the other hand, see a mere chaos of miscellaneous points, a ' big, blooming, buzzing confusion,' as James thought. If there is some compact bright mass of colour in his field of view, such as a face bending over his crib, this probably stands out as a figure from the general background. The baby cannot be supposed to see the face accurately, nor to have any notion what that blotch is, but at least, so the Gestalt psychologists

[1] W. Köhler, *Gestalt Psychology* (Boni & Liveright, 1929), ch. v.

believe, he singles out the face as a compact visual unit, and so makes an important start toward coming to know the face. If it were no easier for him to see the compact figure as a unit than to lump together miscellaneous points from all over the field, his progress in knowing objects at sight would be much slower than it actually is.

Figure and ground are not peculiar to the sense of sight. A rhythmical drum beat or the chugging of a motor-boat stands out as a figure against the general background of less distinct noises ; and something moving on the skin stands

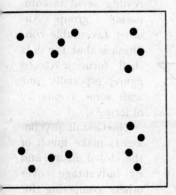 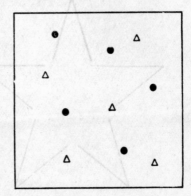

out from the general mass of cutaneous sensations. The facts every one readily admits ; but their psychological significance was overlooked until it was made clear by Edgar Rubin (born 1886), now professor at the University of Copenhagen.[1] Gestalt psychology has seized upon this distinction of figure and ground as a fundamental principle in the organization of experience and behaviour.

Continuing this general line of investigation, and concentrating their efforts largely upon visual material, the Gestalt psychologists seek to discover under what conditions a part of the field stands out as a segregated whole

[1] E. Rubin, *Visuell wahrgenommene Figuren* (Gyldendal, 1921).

from the general mass of stimuli present. Several important factors can be discovered from observing collections of dots scattered irregularly over a field. The dots are seen as falling into groups, and the question is, under what conditions a group is easily formed. One favourable condition is that the dots shall lie near together; neighbouring dots fall readily into the same group. Another favourable condition is similarity of the dots. If the field contains dots of two shapes, or better still of two colours,

those that are alike are readily seen as composing a group. Another favourable condition is that the dots shall form a closed figure, especially one with some regularity of form.[1]

The Gestalt psychologists make much of the closed figure and its advantage over others competing for notice. If a figure is drawn with one or more small gaps in it, these gaps are apt to be overlooked in looking at the figure, or, if not overlooked, disregarded as unimportant. Sometimes, indeed, they catch the eye and stand out as the important thing in the figure. On the whole, the natural tendency seems to be to close up gaps. Instead of explaining this tendency as the result of experience with numerous whole objects, the Gestalt psychologists believe that it represents the inner brain dynamics in receiving a mass of stimuli from the eye. They think of the brain process as tending

[1] M. Wertheimer, *Psychologische Forschung*, 1923, vol. iii. pp. 106–23.

to spread across a gap. With the gap, there is a condition of unbalanced tensions; but closing the gap brings equilibrium. The reception process in the brain gravitates toward a condition of equilibrium, balance, or minimum tension, just as other continuous physical systems do—drops of water, soap bubbles, or electric networks. The brain does not respond with equal readiness and fidelity to all figures, but it does respond to a figure as a whole, and so the seeing of figures is not acquired but inherent in the nature of brain activity.

Filling up gaps in figures is paralleled by the tendency to overlook irregularities, and in general to see as ' good ' or ' pregnant ' a figure as possible in what is presented to the eye. In the Gestalt theory, an imperfect figure means unbalanced brain tensions, while a good figure means equilibrium, and therefore the brain response to what is presented gravitates toward completeness, regularity, and perfection of figure.

In considering the process of seeing figures or objects, we should not forget the movements of the eye, the movements of looking straight at an object and of focusing upon it. These movements give better figures than can be had in blurred vision; and our inveterate tendency is so to direct and focus the eyes as to secure the best and clearest figure. Thus the motor activity in seeing is to be regarded as part and parcel of the perceiving process. ' The optical sensorium and motorium cannot be regarded as two independent pieces of apparatus, since for many types of performance they constitute a unitary organ—a physical system—within which separate organic parts may react upon other parts. Accordingly, what happens at one point in the organism is never independent of, or without its influence upon, what is taking place at any other part of the organism.' [1]

[1] K. Koffka, *The Growth of the Mind* (Routledge, 1925), p. 80.

Though the Gestalt psychologists thus devote much of their energies to the investigation of sense perception, this is not because they regard motor activities as falling outside of the field of psychology. It has appeared to them that the study of sensory processes afforded about the best approach to the dynamics of behaviour in general. Also, they are sure that behaviour can never be understood in the least degree without taking account of perceptual processes. You remember that Hunter, the behaviourist, tried to rule out the study of what he called the environment from the study of behaviour. Other sciences, he urged, are devoting their time to the study of the environment ; and the behaviour student may well leave it to them, and concentrate his efforts on the reactions of the organism. Now if it is the environment that is being studied in studies of perception, at least it is the environment as it affects the individual—the environment as the individual takes it in. The Gestalt psychologists hold that it is absurd to study the motor responses of the organism to the environment without considering what the environment is, as the organism gets it. They hold that motor activity is determined by perceptual activity, or, rather, that either taken alone is an artificial fragment, since the organism acts as a whole. Sense perception is embedded in the total activity of the organism ; and motor response is embedded in that same total activity.

GESTALT STUDIES OF BEHAVIOUR

Gestalt psychology dislikes the stimulus-response conception. It objects, first of all, to the idea that behaviour can properly be analysed into stimulus-response units. This objection is in accordance with its general objection to atomism in psychology. It objects to the notion of a bond between stimulus and response, whether provided by nature or drilled in by practice and experience. It objects to Herbert Spencer's theory, accepted by many behaviourists, that an instinct is simply a chain of reflexes ; and it objects to the similar theory that learned behaviour consists of reflexes linked together by the process of ' conditioning.' Moreover, it objects to the loose way in which the term ' stimulus ' is used by many psychologists. A psychologist will speak of a complex object as the stimulus, and of the motor response as being called out directly by this stimulus, disregarding the organization that must occur in sense perception before the mass of discrete stimuli received from the object can be seen as an object at all. In the Gestalt view, the infant does not start life with an assortment of separate reflex movements, which gradually become conditioned and combined into behaviour. The infant starts with behaviour of a fluid and crudely organized sort, and his adjustments to the environment involve organization on the sensory side as well as on the motor, these two being embedded in the total activity of the organism. Moreover, this total activity has from the beginning, and throughout, a character which may well be called purposiveness.

Professor Kurt Lewin (born 1890), of the University of Berlin, is the member of the Gestalt group who is devoting himself specially to the psychology of action. His objection to associations and stimulus-response bonds is not so much that such connexions do not exist, as that they do not bring about action. They are not the sufficient causes of action. He illustrates his point by an illustration from everyday life, critically interpreted.[1]

Suppose I have stuck a letter in my pocket, impressing on myself the necessity of placing it in a letter box when I pass one in the street. I have thus established a bond

[1] K. Lewin, ' Vorsatz, Wille und Bedürfnis,' *Psychologische Forschung*, 1926, vol. vii. p. 335.

between the sight of the letter box, as stimulus, and the response of taking the letter out and posting it. I see a letter box and post the letter. The associationist or stimulus-response psychologist would cite the case, so far, as a good instance of his doctrine. But now it is also according to the association psychology that exercise of this stimulus-response connexion should strengthen it. Therefore, when I reach the second letter box my response of reaching in my pocket for the letter will be even stronger. On the contrary, that tendency is probably all wiped out. When I placed the letter in the first box, I said to myself, ' That's done,' and apparently erased the stimulus-response bond. Lewin urges that the driving force which activated the behaviour was not the bond, nor even the letter box as stimulus, but a tension set up when I placed the letter in my pocket with the intention of posting it. This tension was relieved when the letter was posted, and the bond had no further influence on my behaviour. Had I happened to spy a postman and hand him the letter, that different act would also have relieved the tension.

The behaviour in such cases may be brought under the formula of ' closing the gap,' and so lined up alongside of the tendency to see closed figures ; and probably the brain dynamics of the two processes is much the same. When I put the letter in my pocket I had to leave a gap in my behaviour, a gap which was filled when the letter was posted. Filling the gap brought this particular dynamic system into a state of equilibrium with no more force to influence my behaviour.

When an individual undertakes a task, or embarks upon a performance—even if it be simply a task assigned him as subject in a laboratory experiment—tensions are generated in him which are not relieved till the task is completed. These tensions amount to a ' quasi-need,' analogous to the organic needs, though only temporary. If the subject is interrupted in the midst of his performance, he feels the need of going back to it as soon as the interruption is over ; and if this is not permitted, it sticks in his memory for an hour or two better than similar performances which he has finished. A finished task is done and can be forgotten ; while an interrupted task still has the tension of its quasi-need. The gap has not been closed. On the other hand, if the subject is set at a monotonous task that has no definite end, and left to himself, his quasi-need is soon satisfied. If the experimenter has instructed him to keep it up until he feels he will not do it any longer, he may continue for an hour making an endless series of dots or strokes on sheets of paper, but he is very apt to find goals for himself as he goes along. The end of a line is a goal ; the end of a sheet is a goal, which he will reach before giving up. He strives at one time for speed, at another for regularity. He combines his dots into groups, it may be, and so adds a pinch of sense to the monotonous task. Finally the ' gap ' is more than full, the tension sets away from it, and the subject, though politely urged by the experimenter to continue if he will, breaks off with decision or even with an explosion of rage.[1]

The most generally interesting of all the work of the Gestalt school is Köhler's study of learning in apes.[2] Just before the World War, the Germans established an anthropoid station at Teneriffe in the Canary Islands, and Köhler was sent out there in 1913 to make psychological studies of the chimpanzees. As a German citizen, he was marooned there during the war, and had plenty of time to make a thorough study, which, indeed, he proceeded to do. The problem that he set himself was whether these most intelli-

[1] These studies are from Lewin's pupils : M. Ovsiankina, *Psychologische Forschung*, 1928, vol. xi. pp. 302–79 ; B. Zeigarnik, *ibid.*, 1927, vol. ix. pp. 1–85 ; A. Karsten, *ibid.*, 1928, vol. x. pp. 142–254.
[2] W. Köhler, *The Mentality of Apes* (Harcourt, Brace & Co., 1925)

gent of animals showed any real intelligence. By real intelligence he meant something more than learning by trial and error. He meant insight, in the sense of seeing what one is doing. Thorndike had been convinced by his studies of cats, dogs, and the smaller monkeys that these animals learned by trial and error, i.e. by impulsive action with stamping in of the successful reactions, and stamping out of the unsuccessful, according to the law of effect—a blind process of learning. Though Thorndike's experiments had not extended to the anthropoid apes, the general impression left behind by his work was that learning by trial and error, without anything that would be called either reasoning or insight, was practically the exclusive method of animal learning. Köhler entertained doubts on this matter, and believed that Thorndike's associationist background had led to a false set-up and to false interpretations of the results.

Thorndike had used mazes and puzzle boxes—blind situations, not lying open to the animal's inspection. Thorndike did this so as to give the animals something to learn. If he had left a clear, unimpeded path to the goal, the animals would naturally have gone straight to the goal and there would have been nothing to learn. Köhler agreed that there must always be some obstacle ; the animal must be forced to take some roundabout path, literally or figuratively, in order to reach the goal. But Köhler argued that the animal should nevertheless be able, from the start, to look over the whole situation, so that if he had the power of insight he could solve the problem without blind trial and error. The elements of the situation should all be visible, and the question should be whether the animal could combine them—whether the animal could see the pattern of the situation.

To show what is meant by ' insight,' the simplest instance of it may be described. If a dog is brought into a strange yard, containing a length of fence, and if, while the dog is at the middle of the fence, some food is placed directly in front of him but on the other side of the fence, the dog almost immediately, so Köhler found, makes a dash around the end of the fence to the food. The dog can *see* the way to the food, though it is not a direct path. In a complicated maze, on the other hand, the animal must explore, not being able to see the whole path to the goal. Köhler's chimpanzees solved with ease any problem which consisted literally in a roundabout path to the objective, provided the path were all in clear view.

If, while the chimpanzee was in his cage, a banana was placed outside at too great a distance to be reached directly, but with a string tied to it and laid along the ground to the cage, the chimpanzee would usually pull the string at once. If, however, several strings were laid on the ground, all extending in the general direction of the banana, but only one attached to the banana, the chimpanzee would often make a mistake and pull a wrong string first. A man in the situation presented would have no difficulty in seeing which string connected with the objective, and would get the banana promptly. But the visual picture was a little too complex to yield its pattern instantly to the chimpanzee.

A stick, lying right at hand, is readily adopted as a means of poking in a banana which lies too far to be reached by the unaided hand. If the stick is placed at the back of the cage, though the animal may see it and handle it as he moves about the cage, he is unlikely at first to use it as a poker. Apparently, his failure in the latter case is due to the absence of a compact visual pattern of stick and banana. The 'gap' in the situation is too large to be bridged instantly. After much use of sticks for hauling in objects, however, this difficulty is overcome.

Similarly, the chimpanzees found it rather easy to use a box to reach food placed too high to reach by jumping, and to fetch the box to the right point if it were not too far away ; but the use of two boxes, one piled on the other to reach to a still higher objective, was a much more difficult problem, though solved by several of the animals. They showed little insight in the matter of stability of construction, but would pile the boxes carelessly one on another, depending largely on their own agility to reach the objective before their structure collapsed.

The prize performance was that of one chimpanzee, the most intelligent of the group tested, who learned to join two pieces of bamboo into a long stick, and with it reached objectives that were beyond the reach of either piece alone. The solution came after an hour of trial and error behaviour, but was so sudden when it came, attended with such new liveliness after listlessness, and so well remembered the next day, as to leave no doubt in the observer's mind of the genuineness of the insight. The solution did not occur, indeed, as the result of a deliberative process, such as might be expressed by saying, ' I could reach the banana if I had a longer stick. How can I make a longer stick out of what I have ? ' But neither did it occur as an incident in the midst of impulsive motor behaviour. It seemed to occur in the field of sense perception, and to consist literally in *seeing* a combination or pattern of objects.

INSIGHT ESSENTIAL IN LEARNING ACCORDING TO GESTALT PSYCHOLOGY

We have found the Gestalt psychologists fully as eager to scrap the older—though not really old—descriptions of behaviour as to leave behind the older way of describing conscious experience. Nowhere are they more radically at issue with previously accepted doctrines than on the theory of learning. The trend of psychological theory, from the day of Ebbinghaus on, had been in the direction of a mechanical conception of learning. We must not forget, to be sure, the results of G. E. Müller, showing the importance of groupings, relationships, and meanings in memorizing numbers and similar material. But on the other side, the work of Pavlov, and the enthusiasm with which psychologists took up the idea of the conditioned reflex, reinforced the old associationist conception of learning as consisting of linkages formed between separate ideas, or, in more modern terms, between stimuli and responses. The Gestalt psychology is the chief opponent of associationism. It has no faith in these elementary linkages, whether native or acquired. Not that it dislikes brain mechanics—or dynamics ; but it believes the brain to work in large patterns, by ' closing gaps,' etc., rather than by the operation of nerve paths linking this and that little centre in the brain.

Koffka, in a discussion [1] of the whole subject of learning based largely on the anthropoid studies of Köhler, seems to reach the conclusion that all learning consists in insight, and that Thorndike's supposed learning by trial and error is simply a mistake. You remember that Thorndike had pointed to the gradual improvement shown in his learning curves as evidence against any sudden insight. Koffka re-examines Thorndike's curves, and finds in some of them sudden drops. These occurred at the beginning of the learning of problems which were easy for the animals. Regarding these instances of quick learning, Thorndike had remarked, ' Of course, where the act resulting from the impulse is very simple, very obvious, and very clearly defined, a single experience may make the association perfect, and we have an abrupt descent in the time-curve

[1] K. Koffka, *The Growth of the Mind* (Routledge, 1925), pp. 153-230.

without needing to suppose inference.' [1] Not inference, certainly ; but it may be that what is ' very simple, very obvious, and very clearly defined' to the animal is a situation in which the animal sees just what it has to do. It may not see into the mechanics of a door button, but it may notice that the button is the thing to claw. That would mean insight of a low order.

Koffka implies, however, that there is no learning except through insight. Insight is not simply to be placed alongside of trial and error as an additional mode of learning ; but it is to displace it altogether. The trial and error principle, as Koffka understands it, means in the first place that nothing new can ever be learned, since the trial and error behaviour consists of instinctive responses and all that is achieved by the learning process is the elimination of some of these responses and the fixation of the rest. Nor can there be any aim or direction in the trial and error behaviour ; the animal must simply strike around at random. Insight and intention can play no part in his movement, and the elimination of unsuccessful movements and fixation of the successful ones must go forward ' without any participation on the part of the animal. The animal has not the slightest notion why its behaviour is being modified ; the whole process, in which the successful acts are preserved and the unsuccessful acts gradually eliminated, is purely mechanical. This is the Principle of Trial and Error.' [2] The animals can never come to see or know how they reach the goal. They learn blindly, and cannot, according to the principle of trial and error— as Koffka understands it—even notice the location of the loop or lever which they claw at in the successful response. They do not see the loop or bar as a way or means of escape.

[1] E. L. Thorndike, *Animal Intelligence : Experimental Studies* (The Macmillan Co., 1911), pp. 73-4.

[2] K. Koffka, *The Growth of the Mind*, 1925, p. 155.

I am not sure that Koffka means to attribute all these statements to Thorndike. Rather, he seems to catch Thorndike in occasional involuntary slips into a sensible way of regarding the animal's actions. Logically, Thorndike should have agreed to all the foregoing statements, according to Koffka. Actually, Thorndike often speaks of the animals as reacting to ' sense impressions,' and certainly does not think of them as striking out blindly here and there as if in a trance or blind fit. His description runs as follows : [1]

When put into the box the cat would show evident signs of discomfort and of an impulse to escape from confinement. It tries to squeeze through any opening ; it claws and bites at the bars or wire ; it thrusts its paws out through any opening and claws at everything it reaches ; it continues its efforts when it strikes anything loose and shaky ; it may claw at things within the box. . . .

The cat that is clawing all over the box in her impulsive struggle will probably claw the string or loop or button so as to open the door. And gradually all the other non-successful impulses will be stamped out and the particular impulse leading to the successful act will be stamped in by the resulting pleasure, until, after many trials, the cat will, when put in the box, immediately claw the button or loop in a definite way.

Thorndike's description certainly implies that the animal was responding, not simply to the total situation of confinement in a strange box, but also to particular features of the situation, openings, bars, anything loose and shaky, buttons or loops. Its reactions were directed by visual stimuli, and to some degree it must have seen what it was clawing or biting. How accurately it saw them is another question. In certain experiments, Thorndike moved the

[1] E. L. Thorndike, *Animal Intelligence : Experimental Studies*, 911, pp. 35, 36.

wire loop which had to be pulled to another part of the cage, and the animal learned to respond to it there with little delay. Again, the experimenter replaced the loop by a little platform to be pushed down, placing this where the loop had been ; and the animal had no difficulty in transferring its efforts to the new device in the old place. Thorndike took these results to mean that the animal did not notice the change that had been made in the situation. ' It reacts to a vague, ill-defined sense-impression, undiscriminated and even unperceived in the technical sense of the word. . . . So cats would paw at the place where a loop had been, though none was there.' [1] This last result indicates that the cats did, in some sense, notice the *place* where they had to work in order to get out. Other experiments show that animals very quickly learn locations, and experiments on human learning show that men, as well, learn locations more easily than most things. Now ' insight ' is a relative matter. If you have to get out of a cage by turning a door button, and simply notice where the thing is that you have to manipulate, that is insight of a low order. If you see the button as an obstacle that must be pushed aside to allow the door to move, that is insight of a higher order. If you understand the mechanics of the thing, that is still higher insight.

Insight of a low order may consist simply in the centring of the animal's activity upon the key to the problem. Such is Koffka's way of reading insight into Thorndike's results. He writes : [2]

Even Thorndike's experiments seem to show that the animal not only experiences certain vague total situations, but that in the course of learning this total situation becomes organized. (The loop becomes) . . . ' something to be struck at,' or ' something to be moved.' As such, it comes to occupy the central position in the total phenomenal situation.

---

[1] Thorndike, *op. cit.*, p. 119.   [2] Koffka, *op. cit.*, p. 172.

. . . If, now, the loop becomes the central feature of the situation, this shows that neither it nor the movements made with it are without significance to the animal ; for the animal has in some way connected its action upon the loop with the food outside the cage. The theory of an entirely meaningless learning is simply untenable.

The stress of Gestalt psychology is on the perceptual factor in learning. Learning means doing something new. The newness cannot be understood by examining the motor performance alone, for the newness consists in a reorganization of the situation, so as to bridge the gap between the situation as it is and the goal. The gap is bridged by seeing the situation as a pattern including and leading to the goal.

Yet another experiment on animal learning is believed to support the Gestalt conception. Let an animal first be trained to find his food in that one of two boxes which is marked by a patch of a certain shade of grey. Suppose two boxes are always placed before him, A and B, of which A is marked with a light grey, and B with a medium grey. After the animal has learned to go always to B, box A is removed and box C, marked with a grey still darker than B, is substituted. Will the animal preserve his supposed fixed association, his positive response to B ? As a matter of fact, he goes now to C. He still goes to the darker of the two boxes. What he has learned, then, is not a response to a certain particular grey; he had learned to respond to the lighter-darker pattern by going to the darker side. Whether we can generalize from the behaviour towards shades of grey, and conclude that the animal always responds to patterns or configurations, rather than to separate stimuli, is a question that has not been sufficiently studied. But on the basis of this experiment, it has been argued that all of the older theory of learning must be given up. In particular, Thorndike's laws of learning are held to

9

be now overthrown. One of the American adherents of the Gestalt school [1] has put the matter in this way :

The 'laws' of Thorndike . . . grow out of a number of *assumptions*, among them, first, the assumption that a given isolated stimulus will always and inevitably produce the same response, and, secondly, the assumption that the 'laws' of learning deal with hypothetical units of behaviour designated by the formula S—R. Behaviour thus atomized logically leads us to look for elements in a given situation, and to regard these elements, if found or assumed, as the primary components which we must add together in order to produce and to explain learning.

If you are a reader of Thorndike, you may not find these 'assumptions' familiar. They do not sound specially like the Thorndike you have read. They must come from another man of the same name, namely, a man of straw. The real Thorndike always speaks of 'situation and response,' while the straw Thorndike, as just quoted, atomizes behaviour by looking always for elements in a situation. The real Thorndike makes this kind of a statement.[2]

Behaviour is predictable . . . the same situation will, in the same animal, produce the same response . . . if the same situation produces on two occasions two different responses, the animal must have changed.

The nearest approach I can find in Thorndike's writings to the atomistic conception attributed to him by the Gestalt psychologists is the following:[3]

All learning is analytic. (1) The bond formed never leads from absolutely the entire situation or state of affairs at the

---

[1] M. H. Lewis, *Journal of Experimental Psychology*, 1930, vol. xiii. pp. 61–75.

[2] Thorndike, *op. cit.*, p. 241.

[3] E. L. Thorndike, *Educational Psychology*, vol. ii. : 'The Psychology of Learning' (Routledge, 1913), pp. 32–5.

moment. (2) Within any bond formed there are always minor bonds from parts of the situation to parts of the response, each of which has a certain degree of independence, so that if a part of the situation occurs in a new context, that part of the response has a certain tendency to appear without its old accompaniments. . . . In the lower animals, and in very young children, the situations act more as gross totals ; and the combination of connexions which we call ' the ' bond between the situation and its response acts more as a unit. . . . In all save stupid men, the training given by modern life results in the formation of an enormous number of bonds with separate elements of situations.

Such a view is far from atomism. It is laid down as a basis for understanding how man comes, by training, to respond to such isolated features of a situation as number, shape, or the pitch of tones. It seems also to lay the basis for meeting the very different and even opposite criticism made by Koffka and quoted a few pages back : ' Even Thorndike's experiments seem to show that the animal not only experiences vague total situations, but that in the course of learning this total situation becomes organized.' According to Thorndike, the animal may advance a little way from the primitive global association with the total situation, and man can go much further in the analytic direction. The association is said to be always complex— as it probably is—but nothing is said of its being compounded of atomic elements.

New schools need men of straw to attack. A new school raises a new question which no one has previously tried to answer specifically. The new school takes its side of the new question, and needs somebody to take the opposite side in the debate which it is staging. It selects the most available authority, and proceeds to put into his mouth an answer to the new question. He has never given that answer directly, because he has never had the question before him ; but the new school says that he ought in all logic to have given that answer, since it is implied as an underlying assumption in what he has said. So the new school can start the debate with an attack, instead of gently putting forth its new question and its own answer. It is all just a bit of psychology, and probably no well-adjusted psychologist objects to being a man of straw in a first-class debate.

THE THEORY OF LEARNING MORE UNCERTAIN THAN EVER

The present situation regarding the learning process is certainly interesting. We have what is really a three-cornered debate going on. We have a variety of facts, all of which need to be accounted for by an adequate theory ; and we have a choice of theories, none of which has attempted to take care of all of the facts. We have the fact of trial and error learning, with the law of effect put forward in interpretation. We have the fact of the conditioned reflex, with the theory of conditioning as interpretation. And we have the fact of learning by insight, with the theory of tensions bridging the gap as interpretation.

The supporters of each interpretation could make out a plausible case for explaining all the facts in their own way. Supporters of the law of effect could point to the methods used in establishing and extinguishing a conditioned reflex as good evidence that the outcome of the reaction determines whether it is being stamped in or stamped out. With regard to learning by insight, they could point out that a gap can be bridged in different ways, a situation organized in different ways, though only one way succeeds in solving the problem. That is, there can be false insights, promising leads which fail, and which thereupon drop out in favour of the insight which comes through.

Similarly, the Gestalt psychologists might, and probably do, doubt whether at least a minimal degree of insight is not present in even the blindest trial and error ; and with regard to the conditioned reflex, they might query whether the dog did not take the metronome, preliminary to the feeding, for a ' signal ' (as Pavlov himself has often spoken of it), and so have ' tensions ' across the gap between metronome and feeding. Finally, the supporters of conditioning could hold that whatever be the complex situation in which learning occurs, the essential learning consists precisely in conditioning. Neither the concept of conditioning nor that of trial and error really depends on the atomism which the Gestalt psychologists so greatly dislike. As our facts become more numerous and more precise, and their relationships better seen, we may find that the contributions of the different schools all have their place in a comprehensive theory of learning.

As matters stand to-day, we can certainly recognize in the Gestalt psychology a strong and valuable addition to the varieties of psychology. Where the existentialists are interested in sensory analysis, and the behaviourists in motor performances, the Gestalt group stress the importance of the topic that has usually been called perception, neglected by the behaviourists and handled very meagrely by the existentialists. There is probably profound truth in their contention that besides sensations and motor responses and bonds between them—besides and including all these—there is the process of dynamic organization. I have given you but a sketchy introduction to their psychology, but I think you will agree that they bring in a fresh point of view that is well worthy of your continued attention.

CHAPTER V

PSYCHO-ANALYSIS AND RELATED SCHOOLS

WE now come to a school of psychology which did not, like those we have studied, originate in psychology itself—at least, not within ' academic ' psychology—but grew out of medical practice. In a broad sense, it is a school of psychiatry. But it has built so impressive a structure of psychological theory about its practice as to challenge the attention and excite the interest of all psychologists. It may be called a psychology of behaviour, though it is as far as possible removed from behaviouristic methods and concepts. It sometimes uses the name ' depth psychology,' because of its concern with what lies in the unconscious depths of the individual's life. It has sometimes called itself ' feeling psychology,' as marking its revolt against the intellectualistic emphasis of nineteenth-century psychology. It has little use for the academic psychology of the laboratory, or for the animal experiments or for the mental tests that have occupied psychologists so largely. None of these lines of study reach the ' depths,' nor afford much practical guidance in medical practice. Its revolt against the academic psychology, then, consists mostly in ignoring it.

As a movement within psychiatry, psycho-analysis was a revolt against the dominant ' somatic ' tendency of the nineteenth century, and a springing into new life of the ' psychic ' tendency. Just when psychology was becoming more somatic, psychiatry started in earnest to be psychic. Convinced that brain lesions were not to be found in some types of abnormal persons, psychiatry began seeking causes of maladjustment in the individual's mental life, in his faulty habits of thought and action, in his weakness of will, in his suggestibility, in his lack of emotional balance. The history of this development is fascinating, but is a story by itself. It is bound up with the history of hypnotism, which, introduced to scientific and medical attention in 1780 by Mesmer—and hence long known as mesmerism—led a chequered career for a century, being associated with much charlatanism and almost universally rejected by the medical profession until the days of the famous rival schools of Paris and of Nancy, in the sixties, seventies, and eighties of the last century. The Paris school was dominated by Charcot (1825–1893), the leading neurologist of his day, a striking personality and a great teacher. Charcot found that individuals who could be deeply hypnotized were subject to fits of hysteria, and used this fact for the understanding and treatment of hysteria, as well as for indicating what to his mind was the nature of hypnosis. It was, he believed, a peculiar pathological state of the organism. In this view he was opposed by the Nancy school, who taught that mild hypnosis could be induced in nearly all normal subjects, being simply a passive and receptive state produced by suggestion. They used it in the treatment of nervous conditions. The strife between these two rival French schools was very keen.

Charcot had many pupils who became prominent in the study of the neuroses. Morton Prince of Boston (1854–1929) used hypnosis and similar procedures in the treatment of multiple or dissociated personality, and is well known to psychologists for his conception of the 'co-conscious,' and for his experiments on split consciousness. Pierre Janet of Paris (born 1859) was also interested in unconscious mental performances, or, as he called them, mental automatisms. In the nineties and later, he devoted himself intensively to the study and treatment of the neuroses. He developed Charcot's use of hypnosis in hysteria, and found that under hypnosis an hysterical patient could recall events that were inaccessible in the waking condition. An emotional shock, though entirely forgotten in the waking condition, would be easily remembered and fully described during hypnosis. Moreover, if during hypnosis suggestions were made by the physician to the effect that ‘that's all past and gone now,’ the hysterical symptoms connected with the emotional shock disappeared. Janet went on to study other types of neurosis, the phobias and obsessions, which he grouped under the inclusive name of psychasthenia, and treated by re-education. His conception of the neuroses is that they are due to a state of lowered mental tension, which prevents the subject from getting up sufficient energy of will and action to overcome the difficulties of life. Given this primary condition of insufficient tension (or voltage, we might say), particular neurotic fears, obsessions, paralyses, etc., develop by mental derivation from the general feeling of insufficiency. Janet's work, slightly antedating psycho-analysis, was beginning to exert considerable influence both in psychology and in psychiatric practice, when it was overtaken by the more dramatic conceptions of Freud and rather thrown into the shade.

Such, then, was the background from which psychoanalysis emerged—a general background of somatic psychiatry, with energetic efforts toward a psychology of the neuroses just being undertaken.

FREUD'S EARLY STRUGGLES

Sigmund Freud was born in 1856 in what is now Czechoslovakia, but has lived in Vienna since his early years.

Attending the University, he studied medicine, and became especially interested in the scientific side of it. He worked for six years in the physiological laboratory, but since he had no immediate prospect of earning his livelihood in that science, he decided to go into medical practice. About 1881, he switched from the physiological laboratory to the hospital, but still continued specializing on the nervous system, its anatomy and organic diseases, such as paralysis and brain injuries. At that time in Vienna there was little knowledge of the neuroses, and little effort to give them medical treatment. The fame of Charcot was heard from the distance, and in 1885 Freud went over to Paris and studied with him for a year. He was much impressed by Charcot's use of hypnosis as a method of treating hysteria. He was also struck by hearing Charcot remark that in all cases of neurosis there was some trouble in the individual's sex life—' always, always '—if you only looked deeply enough. If that were true, Freud wondered, why did Charcot not make use of the fact in his theory and treatment ? The question remained in Freud's mind and bore fruit later.

In 1886, then, Freud returned to Vienna and started active practice on neurotic conditions, especially on hysteria. He used hypnosis as his chief method of treatment, but soon found difficulties with the method. One difficulty was that many neurotic patients could not be hypnotized. Another was that, even when he succeeded in hypnotizing a patient, he could not always effect a cure by its means. This indifferent success that he was meeting led him to make another pilgrimage into France, this time to examine the work of the Nancy school, which claimed to hypnotize practically all comers, and to have much success with curative suggestions under hypnosis. He was somewhat disappointed to be informed by the physicians of this school that their success was not by any means so good with private patients as with the charity patients in the clinic. The private patients were too intelligent or too sophisticated to get full value from the curative suggestions. Freud returned to Vienna and continued work with hypnotic treatment, on private patients, and with only moderate success. He hoped for some better method.

Now enters the story a man from whom Freud probably learned more than from either Charcot or the Nancy school. This was Josef Breuer (born 1842), a Viennese physician who, like Freud, had begun as a physiologist and later shifted to medical practice. He had made important physiological discoveries, and his theory of the semicircular canals is still accepted. Freud and Breuer were old friends and now began to co-operate in their study of the neuroses. It so happened that Breuer was working out a new method of treatment that had originally been suggested to him by one of his patients, a woman who came to him suffering from hysteria. Breuer, as was his custom, had used hypnosis in treating her, and she had found that if he simply allowed her, while hypnotized, to ' talk out ' her emotional difficulties, she was better afterwards. Under hypnosis, she could remember otherwise forgotten events connected with her emotional life, and when she had told the physician about them, she felt relieved and her hysterical symptoms were less intense afterwards. Breuer therefore continued this ' talking out treatment ' and she was finally so much improved as to resume her normal life. Breuer and Freud tried out this new method on other patients with some success and published their results in 1893 and 1895. The new method, so far, used hypnosis combined with the ' talking out.' Almost simultaneously with Breuer and Freud, Janet published some studies of hysteria in which he showed that hypnosis could be used for tapping the patient's memory and discovering the origin of the symptoms. Janet's method was thus identical with that of Breuer and Freud, except that the latter emphasized the curative effect of the mere talking out, if sufficiently continued. They called their new method that of mental catharsis, because it operated to eliminate sources of disturbance from the system. They also used the term abreaction, with the sense that talking out the trouble afforded an expression or outlet for the pent-up emotion and thus removed it. It seemed that the events causing shame or similar emotional disturbance had been violently repressed by the subject, and so made 'unconscious' or forgotten as far as the waking state was concerned, but under hypnosis were revived and abreacted.

Shortly after this promising beginning, Breuer, for some reason that he did not explain, became dissatisfied with the new method and discontinued it, leaving Freud to carry on alone. Later, the reason for Breuer's defection became clear. One of his women patients, when the long series of treatments was about to terminate, declared that she could not part from him because she had fallen violently in love with him. This unexpected abreaction disconcerted Breuer, and he concluded that the new method was dangerous to the practitioner, and made it difficult for him to maintain the purely medical attitude. Freud soon ran into the same difficulty, but was not so easily disturbed. Pondering over the psychology of the matter, he concluded that it was not his own personality that was attracting these women, but that he was simply taken as a substitute, or surrogate, for the original object of their love. The love was transferred to him. If he, for his part, could continue to treat them while maintaining an impersonal attitude, he might even utilize this transference in the cure. It was years before the full theory of transference and the technique for managing it were worked out, but in time it came to hold a predominant place in the whole theory and practice.

Left to himself, Freud soon dropped hypnosis and continued the talking out method without it. Of the hypnotic method, he kept as much as this, that he had his subject assume a reclining position and relax. But instead of going on to induce a drowsy state or to make any suggestions, he simply instructed the subject, while remaining relaxed, to dwell on his troubles and their cause and tell everything that came into his mind. He called this the method of free association, though the association demanded of the subject was not completely free. Some measure of control was exerted by the requirement that the subject must stick to his personal affairs and troubles. He was not to drift into general conversation. But Freud's idea of free association was that the brakes should be taken off, and no repression or censorship exerted on whatever memories might arise in the patient's mind. ' If what comes up is trivial, tell it just the same ; if it is embarrassing, let it come.' Relaxation plus this free association was Freud's substitute for hypnosis. Though it was a slower process, it worked with more subjects and, he believed, led to a more thorough catharsis.

However, this process of analysis of a patient's trouble by direct attack was undeniably slow, and Freud was on the alert for some flank attack upon the unconscious that would catch it off its guard. The patient's dreams, he soon found, afforded such a line of attack. The patient recounts a dream of the night before, and, under the analyst's direction, lets his mind play freely about each item of the dream by the process of free association. Each item of the dream is followed up remorselessly, in the hope of finding significant memories which will fit together and reveal the complex from which the subject is suffering. This dream analysis, invented by Freud in the nineties still remains an important part of psycho-analytic technique. His extensive observations and theories regarding dreams were given to the world in his book, *The Interpretation of Dreams* (published in German in 1900). This book revealed its author as an important contributor to general psychology. To his followers, it appeared as the dawn of the true scientific psychology of the future. He followed the dream book shortly by a fascinating *Psychopathology of Everyday Life* (first German edition, 1901), in which he analyses slips of the tongue or of memory and all sorts of lapses, and shows how they may be used to reveal unconscious complexes ; and in 1905 his *Wit in Relation to the Unconscious* further developed his idea as to the part played by suppressed desires in what we are pleased to call normal life. From about 1900 on, then, psycho-analysis has meant not only a technique for the treatment of the neuroses, but a well-defined psychological theory.

The suppressed desires and complexes that Freud was finding in his analyses of neurotic symptoms, of dreams, of lapses, and of wit were predominantly of a sexual nature. Not only was Charcot's conversational remark confirmed, that sex disturbances were present in all cases of neurosis ; but Freud held that repressed sex desires—repressed because in conflict with the requirements of society—were present in normal people as well, and were responsible for peculiarities of behaviour which at first sight had no possible relation to sex. Partly because of his emphasis on this matter of sex, and partly from the radical and paradoxical nature of many of his theories, his psychology was by no means received calmly by a waiting world. It was accepted with enthusiasm by a few, and violently rejected by the majority. It appeared to some as almost a divine revelation, and to others as a diabolical pseudo-science. With the progress of the years and decades, the atmosphere has cleared somewhat ; both adherents and opponents have become more discriminating ; and the Freudian psychology is now generally regarded, we may safely say, as an important contribution to our growing science, though not as the final and exclusive gospel. Freud himself, even up to an advanced age, has continued to develop and modify his views, though he has not found it necessary to retract many major conclusions which he reached in the early days.

Among neurological practitioners, Freud began to have followers soon after 1900, and gathered a small circle about him in Vienna. Adherents in other countries, especially Switzerland, began to communicate with him, and by 1908 it was feasible to hold an international congress of psycho-analysts. But the expansion of the psychoanalytic group did not proceed far without some internal dissension. The Swiss analysts developed along somewhat independent lines and broke away from close adherence to Freud. Among the Viennese, some of the bolder spirits also broke away. The net result was that from about 1912 there have been several sub-schools under the general psycho-analytic school. The name, psychoanalysis, properly belongs to Freud ; but in a general way the ' analytic psychology ' of Jung and the ' individual psychology ' of Adler are varieties of psycho-analysis, both as methods of neurological treatment and as psychological theories. Freud insists, however, that both Jung and Adler read themselves out of psycho-analysis by rejecting the paramount importance of sex desire in the neuroses and in life generally. We shall return to Jung and Adler after fuller consideration of Freud's own work.

FURTHER DEVELOPMENTS IN PSYCHO-ANALYTIC PRACTICE

Before attempting any connected account of Freud's psychological theory, we should notice the further development of the psycho-analytic treatment. There soon arose the idea among psycho-analysts that certain objects were regular symbols for definite sexual objects and processes. As soon as the patient reported dreaming of these objects, the analyst knew at once the nature of the underlying complex. By use of these fixed symbols, much time would have been saved in the protracted process of analysis, except for the principle, fundamental in Freud's system, that the patient needs, not simply to be told what his trouble is, but to revive his original trouble-causing experiences, and to relieve his complex at the conscious level. Fixed symbols, then, though playing a prominent rôle for a time, later fell into the background.

Equipped with his new methods of free association and dream analysis, Freud proceeded to treat many neurotic individuals with considerable success. He was able to revive experiences that had been repressed, and to clear away hysterical paralyses and anæsthesias and neurotic fears and inhibitions of various sorts. But it occasionally happened that cases dismissed as cured came back after a time with slightly different complaints. That has been the experience of all physicians who attempted to cure the neuroses. But Freud, as usual with him, far from being baffled, remained confident of the value of his methods, and concluded that he had not pushed his analysis far enough. He had, he thought, penetrated the outer layers of the neurosis but not reached its core. It was best, then, to go further back in the patient's life. As his experience increased, he sought to go further and further back in his analysis of the individual. At first satisfied on uncovering a complex of recent date, he later concluded that the recent complex was an outgrowth of an earlier one, which still remained in the subject's unconscious and was likely to cause further trouble.

At first he assumed that the original complex was the

result of some particular emotional shock that the patient had received—as was believed by Breuer and by Charcot. Therefore, he probed further and further back in the subject's forgotten memories to find the episode that had started the trouble. Many of the hysteric women who consulted him were brought by dream analysis to recall emotional shocks from childhood. They recalled being sexually attacked or seduced by their fathers, uncles, or older brothers. Freud, himself rather shocked by the apparent frequency of such occurrences, took occasion to check up some of these stories, and found that they were imaginary. This spurious result of his dream analysis did baffle him for a time, but he soon recovered. What the patient had remembered, he concluded, was some daydream or phantasy of childhood or early youth, and, though not objectively a fact, the fancied episode was real to the patient and just as important in the patient's life history as if it had been an objective event. Further, he concluded that the phantasy had embodied a childish wish of the subject. The daydream of later childhood pointed back to an unfulfilled wish of earlier childhood. If he could push his analysis back to that wish of early childhood, he would have reached the core of the adult's difficulties in life. If, through dream analysis, he could get the subject to revive the lost memories of early childhood and to live over the wishes of that period, he might hope for a radical cure of the neurosis.

Push the analysis back to early childhood ? But that is a practical impossibility, if it means that the individual, as the result of any amount of dream analysis, etc., is to remember the events of the first few years of life with any completeness. In spite of Freud's dictum that nothing ever experienced is ever absolutely forgotten, and that everything would come back if the resistances were sufficiently removed, diligent efforts never succeed in bringing back more than a few scraps of that early experience. However—it may be that the intellectual memory of the early events is not the essential requirement. What is needed may be, rather, the revival of the emotional attitude of early childhood. Make the individual a little child again, emotionally. Even a very scrappy recall of early events may suffice to revive the child's desires and attitude. Such, as I understand it, is Freud's mature conception of what he accomplishes by analysis.

When the subject thus revives his early emotional attitude, without any full revival of the events, objects, and persons that played a part in his infantile drama, the door is thrown wide open to transference. The subject finds a present object for his revived emotions, and that object is the analyst. So far at least as the child's father was the object of his or her love or defiance, so far the analyst as a father substitute becomes the object of the transferred emotion. At certain stages in the progress of the analysis, the subject shows an exaggerated enthusiasm and love for the analyst, while at other stages he may show an extreme distrust and even hate. Both the positive and the negative transference reveal phases of the early attitude toward the father. As the analysis approaches its goal, positive transference is all to the fore. The patient would be left with a childish dependence on the analyst unless a further step were taken, consisting in the weaning of the patient from his transference. Through the transference, the child's desires have been lured out of the unconscious and freed from their childish objects. They must not be allowed to remain fixed upon the analyst, but the patient must be helped to find an outlet for them in harmony with the conditions of his adult life. The analyst must finally withdraw from the drama and leave the patient able to carry his part alone.

Thus by a characteristic stroke of genius of one who was

10

not only a fertile theorist but also in close contact with the actualities of his work, the two great difficulties of psycho-analysis were made to contribute to its success. Free association, which could accomplish relatively little toward a factual reconstruction of early events, was utilized for the emotional revival. And transference, which had threatened to wreck the whole procedure, was made the prime means of success.

Freud himself has given a brief outline of the development of his method. In one of his later writings [1] he distinguishes three stages in his progress.

At first the endeavours of the analytic physician were confined to divining the unconscious of which his patient was unaware, effecting a synthesis of its components and communicating it at the right time. . . .

Since the therapeutic task was not thereby accomplished, the next aim was to compel the patient to confirm the recon-struction through his own memory. In this endeavour the chief emphasis was on the resistances of the patient ; the art now lay in unveiling these as soon as possible, in calling the patient's attention to them, and . . . teaching him to abandon the resistances.

It became increasingly clear, however, that the aim in view, the bringing into consciousness of the unconscious, was not fully attainable by this method either. The patient cannot recall all of what lies repressed, perhaps not even the essential part of it. . . . He is obliged rather to *repeat* as a current experience what is repressed. . . . As a rule the physician cannot spare the patient this phase of the cure ; he must let him live through a certain fragment of his forgotten life.

From this account of the procedure of the competent psycho-analyst, it is clearly no job for the amateur. The analyst, Freud contends,[2] needs at least two years of

[1] S. Freud, *Beyond the Pleasure Principle* (Boni & Liveright, 1922), pp. 17–18.

[2] S. Freud, *The Problem of Lay-Analyses* (Brentano's, 1927), p. 136.

intensive study and supervised practice, before starting practice on his own account. The medical schools at the present time contribute no appreciable part of this training. They teach many subjects for which the psycho-analyst has no use in his practice ; they leave out certain subjects, such as ethnology and the history of civilization, mythology, the psychology of religion, folk-lore, and literature, besides the all-important psychology of the unconscious, or depth psychology ; and they train the medical student rather against than for psycho-analysis, by giving him respect only for the objective and physical causes of disease. A medical graduate who assumes that he is qualified to take a fling at psycho-analytic treatment comes dangerously near to being a quack. Consequently, in view of the great need for qualified psycho-analysts, Freud continues, it is not economically feasible to limit the practice of psycho-analysis to the medical profession. The first step in the intensive training of the analyst is for him to be analysed himself. Only one who has been freed from his own repressed complexes can deal with those of another person. Otherwise his own complexes will crop up during the analysis, and the transference, instead of being exclusively from patient to analyst, will occur in the other direction as well, and we shall have a personal and not an impersonal situation. Psycho-analysis, Freud hopes, will prove of great value in the early handling of maladjustments in childhood and youth.

FREUD'S PSYCHOLOGY

Thus far, we have been following the development of psycho-analysis as a method of treatment of the neuroses, and as a school or movement, and have left Freud's psychological theories in the background. It is not altogether easy to give a statement of Freud's facts, with no admixture of the theories, for the facts are usually put forth clothed in the garb of the theory.

Freud himself has given a concise statement of his main facts.[1]

> The psycho-analytic theory endeavours to explain two experiences, which result in a striking and unexpected manner during the attempt to trace back the morbid symptoms of a neurotic to their source in his life-history ; viz. the facts of transference and of resistance.

The fact of transference has already been sufficiently set forth, though it must be said that, in reality, the facts are the positive and negative emotional attitudes toward the analyst that are shown by the patient during the course of the analysis. That these attitudes are 'transferred' to the analyst from their original objects contains a large element of theory. The fact of resistance is definitely a fact, in the sense that the patient avoids complete frankness in telling his experiences to the analyst. Some memories which come up during free association are 'too trivial' to tell ; others he would 'rather not' tell. But the resistance goes beyond this conscious censorship, for often a memory which is finally recovered and recognized by the patient hangs fire in a very suspicious way. It is approached time and again, but veered away from, the subject not being able quite to recall it, but as it finally comes out clearly and fully, it must evidently have been present in the subject's memory all the time. To conclude that it has been kept back by an unconscious resistance, rather than by imperfections of the associative apparatus, again contains an element of theory. It will be seen, then, that even Freud's basal facts are already tinged with theory. They are interpretations of the facts of the subject's behaviour during analysis, interpretations which fit the behaviour so

[1] S. Freud, *The History of the Psycho-analytic Movement* (Nervous & Mental Disease Publishing Co., 1917), p. 9.

neatly that the analyst is almost forced into them.   Yet these interpretations may be wrong or only partially in accordance with the facts.

In the realm of theory, but still very close to the facts, Freud places repression and infantile sexuality. He writes: [1]

The theory of repression is the main pillar upon which rests the edifice of psycho-analysis. It is really the most essential part of it, and is itself nothing other than the theoretical expression of an experience which can be repeated at pleasure whenever one analyses a neurotic patient without the aid of hypnosis. One is then confronted with a resistance which opposes the analytic work by causing a failure of memory in order to block it. . . .

Just such an acquisition . . . (a theoretical extract from very numerous experiences) . . . but of much later days, is the theory of the infantile sexuality. . . . At first it was only noticed that the effect of actual impressions had to be traced back to the past. . . . The tracks led still further back into childhood and into its earliest years . . . to imaginary traumas. . . . This was soon followed by the conviction that these phantasies serve to hide the auto-erotic activities of the early years of childhood . . . and now the whole sexual life of the child made its appearance behind these phantasies. . . . Years later, my discoveries were successfully confirmed for the greater part by direct observation and analyses of children of very early years.

Repression and infantile sexuality, though spoken of here as theories rather than as facts, are not regarded by Freud as speculative in the least. They seem to him theories that are abundantly confirmed by the psycho-analyst's daily experience with his patients, and that are practically forced upon him. They are, at any rate, interpretations which he finds extremely convenient both in his own thinking and in expounding matters to his patients. If we put the two theories together, we have in a nutshell the fundamentals of Freud's psychology

[1] Freud, *op. cit.*, pp. 9-11.

Repressed infantile sexuality—we see at once that the three words could not be reduced anyhow to two, and that the edifice stands on three pillars instead of two. The importance of repression, the importance of sex desire, and the importance of the infantile period, are Freud's three main emphases.

We should take careful note of what Freud has many times repeated, that his theory does not pretend to cover the whole of mental life, but that it specifically aims to explain what all other theories have had to leave obscure. His is a theory of dreams and lapses, but particularly of the neuroses. A neurosis originates in repressed infantile sexuality—that is his main proposition. However, repressed infantile sexuality is not peculiar to those individuals who have a neurosis at some time in their lives, but is present in all and a factor in the life of all.

If we could discover the methods by which so productive a thinker as Freud reaches his views and theories, it would be a valuable bit of psychology. Probably we can go only a little way in that direction. We notice that when he started his study of neurotic patients, he already had a background of ten years of scientific work. From boyhood he had been an eager and brilliant student, with an intellectual and even scientific bent. Yet I should not say, in view of all his writings, that his temper is exactly that of the scientific man. He appears more as a seer than as an investigator, certainly more as a fertile inventor of hypotheses than as a cold-blooded tester of hypotheses. He seems to have followed a maxim which he received from Charcot, to immerse himself in the facts, especially the baffling facts, in the hope that illumination would come. When illumination did come, as it evidently came often to Freud, it came with great force and assurance, and appeared to him as much more than a hypothesis for further testing. As you read Freud's books, you are struck with the abundance of what, if you think a moment, are seen to be hypotheses. You could find enough of them on certain pages to keep a group of research workers busy for a year testing them out. But Freud passes serenely on and gives you about as many more on the next page. He certainly has a fertile mind.

Freud seems to like paradox. At least, he strives very successfully to escape from the commonplace. He has certain guiding principles which keep his thought away from the obvious. One such guiding principle is that what is forbidden must be desired. Unless people desired to do a thing, prohibitions against that thing could never have arisen in law or custom. What is most strictly forbidden must be very strongly desired. What is abhorrent and shocking must be strongly desired. To kill one's own father is a specially abhorrent deed, and the laws against such conduct have borne extra heavy penalties. There must, then, be a specially strong and common desire to commit this particular crime. Incest, or sex relations between near relatives, is another extra shocking crime. Why should it seem so ? Freud's guiding principle leads him to suppose that the individual must harbour exceedingly strong desires for incest which have to be counteracted by strong condemnation and threats of punishment on the part of society. Hidden, primitive desires can thus be detected and a start made toward depth psychology.

A similar guiding principle is that what is feared is probably desired, the fear being a mask for the desire. Avoidance of pain and direct injury is rational enough, but the fears that we find in civilized life are often queer, when you think of them. Especially is this true of the phobias of neurotic persons. Instead of saying that these are conditioned fears, as the behaviourist would, Freud suspects them of masking unacceptable desires. In the same way, extreme solicitude for some person's welfare may mask an unconscious desire to do him injury.

FREUD'S FUNDAMENTAL ASSUMPTION : MOTIVATION AND PERSISTENT COMPLEXES

Of a different order are certain fundamental assumptions which seem to underlie all of Freud's thinking. Though he himself speaks of repression as the fundamental pillar of psycho-analysis, or, in other passages, of the doctrine of the unconscious (resulting from repressions) as the essence of his depth psychology, yet these assumptions seem even more fundamental.

The chief of these assumptions is that all conduct is motivated. Besides voluntary acts, which are obviously driven by motives or wishes, acts which seem to us involuntary, accidental, or even contrary to our intentions, are nevertheless wish-fulfilling. Such is especially his view of the neuroses. In a valuable summary of the schools of abnormal psychology,[1] McDougall shows that Freud, in distinction from his predecessors, bases his view of the neuroses on motivation. His predecessors, and even his contemporary, Janet, had spoken of the neurosis as an expression of the subject's weakness. Janet spoke of 'low mental tension' as the fundamental weakness of the neurotic, a weakness which was experienced by the subject as a ' feeling of inadequacy,' and out of which the particular phobia or obsession grew as a sort of interpretation by the subject of his own weakness. But Freud interpreted the neuroses as due to desires and their repression. The neurotic symptoms were not for him mere signs of weakness, but were positive wish-fulfilments. If the subject did not want his phobia or paralysis consciously, then

[1] W. McDougall, *Outline of Abnormal Psychology* (Methuen, 1926), pp. 1-29.

he must want it unconsciously. All activity was wish-fulfilling, directly or in some roundabout way.

It would scarcely seem possible that blindness or paralysis —even though 'hysterical' or functional, and not due to organic injury of the brain—should be desired or in any way fulfil a wish of the subject. Janet explains these conditions in accordance with his general notion of low mental tension, as instances of dissociation or 'splitting of consciousness.' The eyes, or the legs, having become connected in the subject's mind with some emotional shock which the subject has not the force to integrate with the main stream of personal existence, split off and escape from the subject's control. Freud's interpretation is quite different. The blindness or paralysis may be a way of escape from some difficult situation ; an invalid is free from responsibilities. But Freud's interpretation is less obvious than this. Here, for example, is a young woman with hysterical paralysis of the legs. A year or two ago, she was her father's nurse during a long illness and was extremely faithful and devoted. She used to lift her help-less father, using her own legs to the utmost. Her life at that time was complicated by the fact that she was in love with a certain young man, and all ready to marry him, except for this unfortunate illness of her father. She could not help wishing, in spite of her devotion, that this illness would terminate, one way or another. Such a desire, though almost overwhelmingly strong, was rejected with horror. She fled from it mentally, or, better, repressed it. But in the unconscious it retained its force, and blindly found a fulfilment through the paralysis. Freud calls this process the ' conversion ' of a desire into the physical symptom. He speaks of the desire as having a certain charge of energy which remains in the system in spite of the repression and is bound to make itself felt in some distorted way, since it is not allowed direct expression.

Let us follow Freud's motivation assumption into some other fields. It is the burden of his *Psychopathology of Everyday Life*. Previous students had classified slips of the tongue or of the pen as errors of omission, of substitution, of transposition, etc., and had spoken vaguely of associations getting off the track. But Freud asks why these lapses do not occur all the time, then, instead of only on certain occasions. It appears to him that his predecessors had treated a lapse as essentially an accident, an event without a cause, and he insists that even in the mental realm every event has a sufficient cause. He analyses the separate instances of lapses, and finds, to his own satisfaction and to the subject's amazement, that each lapse was a wish-fulfilment.

I will cite an instance in which Freud himself had a lapse of memory which he took pains to analyse. Early in his psycho-analytic career he forgot the name of a certain patient who had been in his care. He could not recall the name in spite of the fact that he had treated the patient for a long time. Such a loss of memory appeared strange. Now it happened that this patient had been wrongly diagnosed by Freud and treated for a neurosis when she was really suffering from an ulcer of the stomach. That is the sort of case that the physician likes to erase from his memory, and Freud concluded that he had erased name and all. From such instances, interpreted in his characteristic manner, Freud reached the concept of a motivated forgetting; and though he did not venture to attribute all forgetting to this cause, he came near it in his doctrine that nothing ever known was wholly forgotten or eliminated from the system, though much might be repressed and become practically inaccessible.

Freud shows literary skill and daring in his choice of titles for his books. *The Interpretation of Dreams*, the title of his first great book, announces that here we have Dr.

Freud's dream book. It suggests the old interest, not yet extinguished, in the interpretation of dreams. Of old, the dream was interpreted as having a prophetic significance, but Freud interprets it as a revelation of the individual's past. Previous psychologists had explained dreams simply as disordered trains of uncontrolled association. They had not, to Freud's way of thinking, explained why the individual dreamed of one thing rather than of another ; they left much to accident, and for the rest regarded the dream as just a mechanical running on of the associative machine. But Freud takes his start from the fact that children often dream of having what they wish to have in waking life. I remember that I myself used to dream of finding whole barrels of jackknives— and how disappointed I was to wake up and find the jack-knives gone ! Even as an adult, I have dreamed of finding a penny and then scratching around and finding a sixpence, a shilling, and finally some real money. If any Freudian should hear of this dream, he will surely interpret it to my discredit. Most adult dreams, to be sure, are not obvious wish-fulfilments. But they are wish-fulfilling just the same, says Freud, only that the wishes involved are such as have been repressed. The wish is only symbolically expressed and gratified in the dream. The manifest dream is a distortion of the underlying dream thought and desires. The latent content of the dream, discovered later by the process of free association, is a suppressed wish seeking and finding gratification. The latent content would be abhorrent to the waking individual ; as soon as it started to emerge into consciousness, it would be resisted and sent down again into the unconscious. In sleep the latent content has a little better chance, but still it is censored and only allowed to disport itself in disguise— very complete disguise, usually.

We have followed Freud far enough to make sure, I

believe, of his underlying assumption that all activity is motivated. Motivation is practically the whole of psychology as he sees it. Everything that the experimental psychologists have done in the way of examining the mechanism of dreaming or thinking or memory appears to him of negligible importance. He finds no use for any of it. It proceeds on the assumption, he says, that mental events happen without causes. Such an accusation long puzzled me in view of the fact that experimental psychologists were quite generally studying cause and effect. I finally saw that Freud meant by cause, in the psychological realm, a wish and nothing else. A cause in psychology, he holds, must be a psychic cause, and a psychic cause must be a wish or motive. To speak of an associative machine, or of a brain mechanism, is to drop out of the realm of psychical causation. He sometimes uses the expression, ' full psychic act.' A dream or lapse is a full psychic act. It is, then, essentially the same as a voluntary act, i.e. it is a wish-fulfilment.

I say to you, then, that Freud's assumption of universal psychic causation, his assumption that all activity is motivated, is more fundamental in his psychology than his doctrine of repression. That it is more fundamental becomes clear when we remember how he reaches the doctrine of repression. Repression is the ' theoretical expression of the fact of resistance,' and that fact amounts to the fact that the patient under analysis veers away from certain memories as if afraid of them. Psychologists have explained failures of recall as due to interferences within the associative mechanism, but Freud will have none of such explanations. The failure to recall must be motivated, which means resistance, which in turn points to a previous repression.

The other fundamental assumption that I find in Freud is that the causes, the wishes, are to be sought in the past ;

that the lapse or the dream fulfils not a wish of the moment, but a wish of the past ; that the neurosis has its origin in the past. We have seen how, following this lead, Freud was forced back from the recent past to the first years of childhood. You may say that every one necessarily assumes that the present is explained by the past, but I shall point out shortly that both Jung and Adler differ with Freud on just this point. Freud's assumption of the past as responsible for the present goes beyond the truism that what has happened leaves effects behind it. He means something much more precise than that. He means, or certainly seems to assume as axiomatic, that particular situations once experienced live on in the individual and emerge from time to time as the latent content of dreams and in other ways. More significantly, he means that particular desires once active live on in the individual.

Consider in this connexion the matter of transference. The fact here is the positive or negative emotional attitude of the patient toward the analyst. But to Freud's mind this is the ' fact of transference.' As he senses the fact, old desires, dating from childhood, have persisted and found a new object in the person of the analyst, who is a father substitute. Now suppose that we were interpreting the subject's emotional attitude toward the analyst without assuming the persistence of identical situations and desires from childhood into adult life. In that case, we might say that the present helpless and dependent situation of the subject was similar to his situation as a child, that the place of the analyst in the present situation was like that of the father in the child's situation, and that free association, bringing up some memories of childhood, had revived in the subject some of his childish emotion. Therefore, we might conclude, the subject's situation and condition being similar to that in which he was as a child, he responds to the analyst as he then became habituated to respond to his father. That would not be transference in Freud's sense. There would be no transferring of an identical wish from one object to another. Freud's interpretation may be better, but the point is that it is an interpretation, and that it rests upon the assumption that the wishes of the past live on as the same identical wishes, the new objects which they find from time to time being simply substitutes to which the desires are transferred. What I submit for your judgement, then, is first that transference is not one of Freud's basal facts, but one of his pillars of theory ; and second that this pillar is founded upon the assumption of the permanence of situations and of particular desires.

FREUD'S ASSUMPTION OF THE INHERENT DUALISM OR POLARITY OF THE INDIVIDUAL

We spoke of the three words, ' repressed infantile sexuality,' as embodying the three pillars of Freud's psychology. We have found the assumption of universal motivation underlying the pillar of repression, and the assumption of permanent desires or complexes underlying the ' infantile ' pillar. Shall we yield to temptation and grub for something hidden under the pillar of sexuality ? That would probably be carrying the love for system and order too far. But there is a suggestion of some underlying assumption in the breadth of the sex life as conceived by Freud. He regards thumb-sucking as obviously a form of sex gratification ; also the infant's way of biting things and putting them into his mouth ; also rubbing or being rubbed, stroked or patted ; rhythmical movements of the arms or legs which seem to afford infantile pleasure ; defecation and urination ; looking at things and showing off ; tearing things apart and throwing things down ; and, in short, any activity which affords the infant sensuous and spontaneous pleasure. At a higher level he includes under

sex gratification all affectionate behaviour and comrade-
ship, as well as love for art and music. Whatever we say,
colloquially, that we love or love to do belongs under the
sex impulse. Well, you say, that is simply his use of
terms ; he simply uses sexuality as equivalent to love in
its broadest sense. But we must notice, on the other side,
that Freud objects strenuously to any attempt to de-
sexualize his libido or his sexuality. He insists that
affection is genuinely sexual, and that the baby's thumb-
sucking gives genuine, though rudimentary sex pleasure.
He insists that his conception of sexuality is strict as well
as broad ; and he seems to sense no inconsistency here.
What is thus taken as obvious and self-evident may very
well cover a hidden assumption.

It is just possible that the underlying assumption is that
of a fundamental duality or polarity of mental life. In
many of his theories, Freud gravitates toward a twofold
division. His most familiar dichotomy is that of the
conscious and the unconscious. He speaks also, to be
sure, of the preconscious. But the preconscious belongs
closely with the conscious ; it is what can readily be made
conscious, though not actually conscious at a given moment.
The preconscious is not a half-way point in a continuous
scale extending from the most conscious to the least
conscious, or from the most to the least accessible for
conscious recall. The unconscious is what has been
repressed ; the preconscious, like what is momentarily
conscious, has not been repressed. To treat the preconscious simply as an intermediate degree between the
most conscious and the most unconscious would be to
upset Freud's whole conception of the unconscious. What
he sees here is a polarity, not a continuum.

But what has polarity to do with Freud's peculiar
strict-broad conception of sexuality ? It seems just
possible to me that when Freud, with his underlying

assumption of polarity, envisaged the behaviour and feeling of the child, the line of division that most impressed him was a line between what is done spontaneously and with immediate pleasure, and on the other side what is done of necessity or as a means to an end. All that was done with pleasure struck him as belonging together— intrinsically together and not merely as a convenient classification. The sex feeling and activity of the adult, appearing to be the clearest and fullest manifestation of the loving and pleasurable tendency, furnished the appropriate name for the whole tendency. The child's thumb-sucking, then, is not merely *like* sex activity in some vague and superficial sense, but is really sex activity of an immature sort. It would evidently be quite contrary to Freud's basal assumptions to conceive of human behaviour either as a miscellaneous lot of different types of activity, or as a continuum of degrees of a single activity.

The objection may be raised that Freud did not at first give a name or definition to the pole opposed to sex. In his earlier work, though he said much of repression, resistance, censorship, conflict, and compromise—all of which imply some opposing force that represses the libido—he gave little attention to this opposing force. Sometimes he spoke of the ego or of the ego-tendency, adding at once that he knew little about it, and was sure little could be learned about it till such time as psycho-analysis found it possible to analyse and treat disorders of the ego. Such disorders, he believed, were to be found abundantly in insanity, but thus far insane patients had not proved good subjects for psycho-analysis. For the time, then, the ego had to be left as little more than a name for the tendency opposed to the libido.

He did, however, speak of the polarity of the pleasure principle and the reality principle. By nature man follows the pleasure principle ; he seeks for immediate pleasure, and for the immediate and straight-out gratification of his desires. But he finds himself confronted by the realities of physical nature and of his social environment, which interfere greatly with his desires. He learns to avoid pleasures which bring greater pains, and to defer the gratification of desires in the interests of later and fuller gratification. In his daydreams and in the unconscious he follows the pleasure principle, but his well-ordered waking life is subjected to the reality principle. This duality is primarily between the individual and the environment; but the individual takes over some of the environment into himself, as it were, and so has within himself a force or agency for holding the pleasure impulse in check. But as it exists within the individual the reality principle is rather the servant of the libido than a primal counter urge; and accordingly it did not fully meet Freud's requirement of a fundamental polarity within the individual.

Meanwhile the polarity of ego and libido was not maintaining itself very well. Individuals were found who were in love with themselves. This anomaly of the sex life was named ' narcissism,' after the legendary youth, Narcissus, who fell in love with his own reflection in the brook. There even seemed to be a ' primary narcissism ' in the little child, occurring before he could clearly recognize external persons and things as the objects of his love and the source of his pleasures. At any rate, when the child was rebuffed by any of his love-objects, he tended to withdraw into himself and fasten his libido upon his own ego. If the ego can thus be a love-object, it must belong in part within the realm of the libido, and the self-preservative instincts, at first conceived as opposed to the libido, must after all be alined with it, since they seek to preserve this important love-object. The ego might contain other tendencies not alined with the libido, but it clearly could no longer be regarded as a compact entity or tendency opposed to the libido.

11

Thus enlarged by the inclusion of the self-preserving instincts, the libido or sexual urge was rechristened Eros or the life urge ; and the question remained whether it now included all urges whatever, or whether a polarity could be discovered between it and something else. Several otherwise enigmatical facts led Freud to postulate a ' death instinct ' as the opposite pole. One such fact is the suicidal tendency present in some persons. Another bears the name ' sadism,' referring originally to the sexual anomaly which consists in combining the sexual act with torture of the loved person. The term was extended by Freud to cover all manifestations of cruelty and destructiveness. Then Freud was much impressed with the rhythm of growth and decay in all living creatures and tissues—except, indeed, in the ' potentially immortal' germ cells, which belong, however, to Eros. And besides, as a motivationist, Freud could not help seeing the fact that death is the end of life as meaning that death is the goal of some urge within the individual. The longing for rest or Nirvana was an expression of the death instinct. Destructiveness and cruelty were the same instinct directed outwards upon other persons or objects.

Thus, after long wandering, and by the aid of what he recognizes as speculative thinking, Freud has finally reached a satisfactory and fundamental polarity. He does not intend that this ultimate polarity shall be substituted for all the lesser polarities that he has employed in interpreting concrete instances of human behaviour ; the opposition of ego and libido still holds good in its proper sphere.

A few scattered sentences from Freud's later books may reinforce and clarify what I have been trying to tell you.

At this point opportunity offers of reviewing the gradual development of our Libido theory. The analysis of the transference-neuroses forced on our notice in the first place the opposition between 'sexual instincts' which are directed towards an object and other instincts which we only imperfectly discerned and provisionally described as 'ego-instincts.' Among the latter those which subserve the self-preservation of the individual had the first claim for recognition. . . .

In the course of more deliberate advance it came under psycho-analytic observation how regularly libido is withdrawn from the object and directed towards the ego. . . . The ego took its place as one of the sexual objects and was immediately recognized as the choicest among them. . . . Whereupon the original antithesis between the ego-instincts and the sexual instincts became inadequate. A part of the ego-instincts was recognized as libidinous. . . .

We are venturing on the further step of recognizing the sexual instinct as the Eros, the all-sustaining. . . . Our standpoint was a dualistic one from the beginning, and is so to-day more sharply than before, since we no longer call the contrasting tendencies egoistic and sexual instincts, but life-instincts and death-instincts.[1]

In the works of my later years . . . I have given free rein to the inclination to speculation which I kept down for so long. . . . I have combined the instincts for self-preservation and for the preservation of the species under the concept of *Eros* and have contrasted with it an instinct of death or destruction which works in silence. . . . The picture which life presents to us is the result of the working of Eros and the death-instinct together and against each other.[2]

Over and over again we find on tracing instinctual impulses back that they disclose themselves as derivatives of Eros. If it were not . . . for the sadistic constituents which have attached themselves to Eros, we should have difficulty in holding to our fundamental dualistic point of view. But since we cannot escape that view, we are driven to conclude that the death-instincts are by their nature mute and that the clamour of life proceeds for the most part from Eros. And from the struggle against Eros![3]

---

[1] S. Freud, *Beyond the Pleasure Principle*, 1922, pp. 64–7.
[2] S. Freud, *The Problem of Lay-Analyses*, 1927, pp. 290, 291.
[3] S. Freud, *The Ego and the Id* (Hogarth Press, 1927), p. 66.

FREUD'S EARLIER AND LATER VIEWS ON THE UNCONSCIOUS

In a similar way, Freud was forced into a revision of the conscious-unconscious polarity. At first it seemed clear enough that the ego was conscious, and that the conscious side of life was what repressed desires that were unacceptable to the ego and kept them unconscious by resistance. But it was found that patients undergoing analysis were not aware of their own resistances. Consciously they were offering no resistance to the free recall of past experiences. The resistance was therefore unconscious, and so, doubtless, was the original repression. Thus the ego, in carrying out repression and resistance, was acting unconsciously. The ego, then, is partly conscious and partly unconscious. On the conscious side, it is in contact with the environment, which it perceives by the senses and manipulates by use of the muscles. Conscious pain and pleasure show that it is also in communication with the interior of the organism and of the psyche, though this interior is largely unconscious. The unconscious interior of the psyche consists, dynamically, of the instincts and of particular disturbing desires and experiences that have been repressed. The antithesis here is between what may be called the surface of the psyche, in contact with the environment, and the interior which has no direct contact with the environment. This interior Freud now calls the ' it ' or ' id.' The ego is in contact with the environment, but it has developed out of the id and remains merged with it below, i.e. so far as the ego is unconscious. The id includes the instinctive driving forces of the individual's existence, both the life-instincts and the death-instincts, which take the form of particular desires as they strive out toward the environment and so affect the conscious life. Whenever these particular desires are repressed by the ego, they return into the id. ' The ego tries to mediate between the world and the id, to make the id comply with the world's demands and, by means of muscular activity, to accommodate the world to the id's desires.' [1] The id strives blindly for gratification in accordance with the pleasure principle ; but it has to work through the ego which has learned the reality principle. The ego at first is weak and only slightly developed ; consequently, it meets with many rebuffs in carrying out the behests of the id. It goes after many objects that the environment denies it. When the ego has to give up a love-object, it retains an image of that object and hugs the image to its heart, identifying itself with the object ; and thus the ego grows by appropriating the character of the objects which it has had to renounce. If the ego develops successfully, it becomes coherent and well organized, and adjusted to its environment. The id remains primitive and unorganized.

This drama of the id and the ego is complicated by a third character, the super-ego or ego-ideal. The super-ego corresponds roughly to what we ordinarily call conscience, and the psycho-analyst is forced into adding this actor to the drama by the excessive sense of guilt that many of his patients reveal during analysis. The super-ego has precepts and prohibitions—' thou shalt ' and ' thou shalt not '—which it endeavours to enforce upon the ego. These are not precepts of expediency, derived from the realities of the environment, but categorical imperatives, derived from the inner world, from the id and its internal conflicts. Whereas the ego must be supposed to develop to some extent in all animals through their contest with the environment, the super-ego is peculiar to man and arises in consequence of his protracted childhood and of the delay which his libido must undergo before it can reach its

[1] S. Freud, *The Ego and the Id*, 1927, p. 83.

proper goal in adult sexual life. The super-ego is supposed to have originated in primitive man, and its archaic rudiments are handed down to each individual by inheritance. But for the most part the super-ego originates anew in each child. It originates from the thwarted sex urge of the little child. The sexuality of the child, according to Freud, is true sexuality to the extent that it demands a love-object, typically of the other sex, finding that love-object in one of the parents. Thus arises the 'Oedipus complex,' that most famous of Freud's constructions, which needs to be understood before the origin of the super-ego can be further explained.

Oedipus, the lame hero of Greek legend, as you will recall, was exposed by his father, the king of Thebes, with a spike through his feet, because the oracle predicted that this child should slay his father and marry his mother. He was rescued and adopted by the king of a neighbouring state, and grew to manhood in ignorance of his true parentage and of his predicted fate. On one occasion, however, when he visited the oracle, he was told that he should slay his father and wed his mother. To avoid such a calamity, he remained away from his adopted home, but in his wanderings met his true father, quarrelled with him, and slew him. Continuing, he reached Thebes, where by solving the riddle of the Sphinx he freed Thebes from a long-standing pest and was proclaimed king and given the widowed queen to wife. Years later, after four children had been born to the innocently guilty pair, the truth came out, and poor Oedipus, in despair, put out his eyes. He lived thereafter in the midst of constant misfortunes.

Of this legend, Freud took only the bare outline. Oedipus unwittingly killed his father and married his mother, committing the two crimes of parricide and incest, which, being so abhorrent, must be strongly desired by all. Freud regarded the legend as representing a complex carried around by every man, originating in the boy's love for his mother and rivalry with his father for the mother's love. The boy baby's libido, attaching itself to the mother, is encouraged for a while, but with weaning, with the possible advent of another baby, with punishment and correction, the course of his first true love is not altogether smooth. Meanwhile the boy has attached himself also to his father as his model or ideal, to be imitated in everything. He has identified himself with his father. But he comes to find, to his own chagrin, that he cannot or must not do all that his father does. In particular he cannot and must not love his mother as his father does. He finds his father an interfering rival, and impulsively wishes him out of the way. His adored ideal has become also his hated rival, and his chosen love-object is denied him. Terrible conflict rages within him, and comes to a head, Freud believes, about the fourth or fifth year, when the boy's libido, after passing through its stages of oral and anal gratification, becomes concentrated upon his genital organs. Now he encounters stern opposition from both parents, and further progress in his love life is blocked. Auto-erotic practices are met by threats, more or less brutal, against the offending member. There is nothing left for him but to renounce and repress. This heroic feat he achieves by adopting his ideal into himself. He carries his identification with his father to such a point as to make his own both the positive precept, ' Thou shalt be like thy father,' and the prohibitions, ' Thou shalt not slay thy father nor covet his wife.' These laws, adopted by the boy, are the core of his super-ego.

Such is the simple Oedipus complex and the manner of its repression ; but ordinarily the drama is complicated by the bisexuality of the child, whether boy or girl. The boy's libido may go out to the father as well as to the mother, and the mother be to some extent the ideal later found to be a rival and finally adopted by identification into the self and given a part to play in the super-ego. The boy's identification may even be more with the mother than with the father, so that his character takes on a feminine stamp. The same drama, with all its complications, holds with suitable substitutions for the girl, though it is apt to be vaguer and less dramatic. With the successful overcoming of the Oedipus complex, at about the fifth year, the child's sexual development ceases till puberty. Whether the youth will successfully meet the demands and opportunities of mature love depends in large measure on how successfully as a child he adjusted the Oedipus situation.

If the Oedipus story of the child seems about as mythical as the old Greek legend, we may regard it as a scheme or diagram of the individual's difficulties in life. It cannot be observed directly in the child, though behaviour is observed that can readily be located in the diagram. To the psycho-analyst, the Oedipus idea has practical value largely, I think, because acceptance of this idea by a neurotic patient helps him in overcoming resistances and taking a calm view of his conflicts. If the conflict can be presented as one dating from infancy, it can be approached more objectively by the patient. Freud himself admits in his later works, that the actual picture is much vaguer than the scheme presents it. He writes : [1]

One gets the impression that the simple Oedipus complex is by no means its commonest form, but rather represents a simplification or schematization which, to be sure, is often enough adequate for practical purposes. . . . A boy has not merely an ambivalent attitude towards his father and an affectionate object-relation towards his mother, but at the same time he also behaves like a girl and displays an affectionate feminine attitude to his father and a corresponding hostility

---

[1] S. Freud, *The Ego and the Id*, 1927, pp. 42–3.

and jealousy towards his mother. It is this complicating element introduced by bisexuality that makes it so difficult to obtain a clear view of the facts. . . . It may even be that the ambivalence displayed in the relations to the parents should be attributed entirely to bisexuality and that it is not . . . developed out of an identification in consequence of rivalry.

Now if the boy's rivalry with the father is allowed to drop out of the story, the dramatic clearness is gone. And if 'bisexuality' is understood in accordance with a fairly 'broad' conception of sexuality, it comes down to affectionate responsiveness to persons of either sex. The ambivalent (positive and negative, loving and hating) attitude of the child toward either parent might then be the outcome of the fact that the child is treated not only tenderly but also sternly at times. The blind forces of the id would not need to be introduced, and the whole story, while ringing true, would scarcely belong in depth psychology.

SUMMARY AND APPRECIATION

Universal motivation, permanence of particular desires, and duality or polarity—those were the underlying assumptions which we glimpsed in considering the broad lines of Freud's psychology. If you will allow me to express the second assumption in more generalized terms, we could speak of permanent particular desires as entities, and remind ourselves at the same time of the numerous other entities that play a part in Freud's psychology. Id and ego and super-ego, Eros and the death-instinct, are the entities finally adopted; but all along there have been entities, such as libido and the censor. A particular desire, repressed but remaining the same identical desire though transferred to a new object, has the character of an entity. When Freud assumes that all behaviour is motivated or wish-fulfilling, he assumes also that the motivation proceeds from entities within the individual, entities that desire and have aims, wish-forces. While, then, the super-structure of his psychological system may be summed up in the words, 'repressed infantile sexuality,' the foundation might be suggested by ' polarized wishful entities.'

Whether we have been doing justice to Freud's psychology by thus concentrating our attention on the higher reaches of his theory, fascinating as it is, remains a question. Quite possibly, the more significant Freud is the Freud in close touch with the actualities, the Freud who by his frank persistence in the study of the sex life has done so much to open the door to a rational consideration of personal problems, the Freud whose methods of analysis have been adopted in more or less modified form by child guidance clinics and other agencies seeking to promote good adjustment to life and to forestall the neuroses. Freud's ' mental mechanisms ' or ' defence mechanisms '—better called [1] ' dynamisms,' as there is nothing mechanistic about them—are useful concepts in the psychology of personality. The masking of desire by fear is such a ' dynamism.' Another is the rationalization of an un-acceptable desire. The best known is perhaps ' sublima-tion,' the finding of a socially acceptable outlet for a desire which cannot be allowed direct expression. Exactly how, when, and to what extent sublimation can be achieved remains a question ; but, as in many other instances, Freud's conception serves at least to point to certain facts, usually overlooked, and to stimulate further observation. Like behaviourism, and even more than behaviourism, psycho-analysis has sought to extend its influence into the field of social problems, and has taken on the character of a social movement and almost of a religion.

[1] See W. Healy, A. F. Bronner, and A. M. Bowers, *The Structure and Meaning of Psycho-analysis* (Judge Baker Foundation, 1930), p. 192.

But to appreciate Freud's full importance in the scientific and medical development of the present time, we need to recall that his most serious efforts have been directed, all along, to the understanding and treatment of the neuroses. I suppose it will be agreed that his contributions to this, his chosen field, have been solid and enduring. He has revolutionized the subject by showing that the neurosis is not due, fundamentally, to an emotional shock or trauma from without, but to the patient's awkward attempts to reach some adjustment between his own desires and the conditions of his life ; and further that the neurotic must himself discard his poor adjustment for a better one, while the physician assists through the medium, largely, of the peculiar form that the neurosis takes under the physician's influence, namely, the transference neurosis. Freud does not permit us to think of the individual as yielding like putty to 'environmental pressures,' or as being 'conditioned' to any social situation with perfect readiness. The demands of society encounter opposing demands of the individual, whence arise conflict and the need and difficulty of adjustment. Inasmuch as maladjustments of greater or less seriousness occur in all of us, and as what Freud has discovered regarding the more serious neuroses may hold good of the milder maladjustments as well, his contribution to the psychology of personality is obviously very great.

If my personal opinion of Freud's psychology were sought, I should have to say that I cannot believe his system to be true in any absolute sense, or even to rank with the great scientific theories which co-ordinate existing knowledge and serve as guides to further discovery. With its entities and its dualism, it seems to be retrograde rather than forward-looking. Freud's more limited theories stand on a different footing; they promise to stimulate research, though of course they may be overthrown by the research which they stimulate. Freud's real greatness seems not to lie in the formulas in which he has cast his thinking, so much as in the thinking itself and in the freshness of his approach ; it lies rather in his effectiveness as a pioneer than in the conclusions thus far achieved.

MODIFICATIONS OF PSYCHO-ANALYSIS :
ALFRED ADLER'S ' INDIVIDUAL PSYCHOLOGY '

It was about 1912, some ten years after psycho-analysis had begun to make a stir in the world and to attract adherents, that cleavages appeared within the group that had gathered about Freud. It would have been too much to expect all these energetic young men, however enthusiastic over the bold innovations that Freud had made, to stay exactly where he placed them. Wilhelm Stekel and Fritz Wittels, prominent members of Freud's Vienna group, left it on account of what seem to have been minor differences in methods or theories. Adler and Jung separated, or were separated, from Freud because they taught a different psychology from his.

Alfred Adler of Vienna (born 1870) had attached himself very early to Freud's circle and had probably exerted considerable influence on Freud's earlier conceptions of the ego.' But by 1912, it had become clear that his emphasis on the ego as against the libido was unfitting him for close adherence to Freud. He therefore started a rival school and named it ' Individual Psychology.' Adler had apparently believed from the start that Freud was overemphasizing sexuality. While recognizing the frequency of sex difficulties in the neuroses, Adler thought he saw something more fundamental.

It seemed to him that the fundamental fact in neurosis was a feeling of inferiority. There might be some genuine inferiority of a physical sort, but at any rate there was a feeling of inferiority. Such a feeling cannot be tolerated by any one, for the simple reason that every one has a fundamental will for power, an urge toward dominance and superiority. If an individual finds in himself something inferior or lacking, he is driven to die or else to make himself superior in some way or at least pretend to himself and to others that he is superior. He may truly compensate for his inferiority by well-directed effort, as Demosthenes overcame his stuttering by speaking on the seashore with pebbles in his mouth, becoming the greatest orator of Greece ; or as Roosevelt overcame his frail physique by ranch life and became a ' rough rider ' and explorer. Often the compensation moves away from the point of inferiority as a boy who is weak in his muscles may find he can shine in school and seek his success there. Many a man whose success in life makes us suppose him proud and perfectly sure of himself turns out, if we come to know him intimately, to have suffered from strong feelings of inferiority which he has not entirely overcome. In short, then, Adler regards the self-assertive impulse instead of the sex impulse as the dominant positive force in life, and as the impulse most subject to frustration from the environment and from the individual's own sensitiveness. It is thus the source of achievement on the one hand, and of misconduct and maladjustment on the other.

Where Freud conceived the ego as well-attuned to the reality principle, Adler held that it was specially prone to falsify reality. The phantasies of the individual did not, in his view, consist mainly in imaginary gratifications of the libido, but in easy, because imaginary, ways of escape from the sense of inferiority. The weak individual was likely to invent ' arrangements ' for himself, and to adopt a ' style of life ' or behaviour pattern that enabled him to avoid the demands of the environment and score a success in his own estimation. Such a neurotic individual set for

himself a ' fictive goal ' which meant no real achievement.
As Adler says : [1]

> The problem of every neurosis is, for the patient, the
> difficult maintenance of a style of acting, thinking and per-
> ceiving which distorts and denies the demands of reality. . . .
> As the work of Individual Psychologists has abundantly
> proved, an individual goal of superiority is the determining
> factor in every neurosis, but the goal itself always originates
> in . . . the actual experiences of *inferiority*. . . . ' If I were
> not so anxious, if I were not so ill, I should be able to do as
> well as the others. If my life were not full of terrible diffi-
> culties, I should be the first.' By this attitude a person is
> able still to feel superior. . . . His chief occupation in life is
> to look for difficulties. . . . He does this more to impress
> himself than others, but naturally other people take his
> burdens into account and . . . he wins his way to a privileged
> life, judged by a more lenient standard than others. At the
> same time, he pays the costs of it with his neurosis.

The style of life is adopted by the child within his first
few years, and remains fixed in its main lines. Each individual, then, has a typical goal toward which he tends in
every new situation, especially as he encounters the three
great problems of life, that of social and community life,
that of occupation, and that of love. The style of life is
not forced upon the individual by heredity, but is very
largely determined by the family situation in which the
child finds himself. So, the children of very successful
men are handicapped by hopelessness of attaining anything
as great as their fathers, and are likely to adopt a style of
life which calls for no serious efforts. A child of very poor
parents, but of attractive appearance, may adopt a
begging attitude which persists later in all sorts of situations. The spoiled child adopts as his goal to be the
centre of attention. The hated child has the goal of
escaping to a safe distance. The eldest child adopts the

[1] A. Adler, *Problems of Neurosis* (Cosmopolitan Book Corporation, 1930), pp. 41, 46, 47.

attitude of keeping what he has, a conservative attitude. The second child from the start is behind in the race, and develops the attitude of seeking to surpass. This may be the attitude also of the youngest child, though he is rather likely to develop the attitude of the spoiled child. The only child, never having met competition, assumes that others will serve and he rule. Adler does not mean that the mere position in order of birth determines the child's style of life. But a child is typically born into a certain situation, according as he is oldest or younger, and his attitude toward life, his expectations from life, are likely to be moulded very early by the competitive situation in which he finds himself. Thus Adler, no less than Freud, but in a very different way, emphasizes the family situation as forming the individual.

Adler does not deny the importance of the sex impulse, but he believes it has not the comprehensive importance in the child's life that Freud attached to it. It finds its place in a total scheme or style of living which consists fundamentally in an always present drive toward superiority or at least against inferiority. An analysis of the individual's life and problems which centres everything about the sex urge gives a distorted picture. ' The sexual components cannot even be correctly estimated except in relation to the individual style of life. . . . We can gain insight into the erotic life, with all its waywardness, hesitation, and elusive subtleties, only so far as we grasp the individual's style.' [1] Of the three great problems of life— social life, occupation, love—it is the social problem that the child first encounters ; and his social adjustment as a child is the prototype of his approach to the other problems as they arise. If the child's social attitude is one of courage and interest in other people, optimistic both in giving and receiving, he can later take up the sex impulse

[1] A. Adler, *Problems of Neurosis*, 1930, p. 93.

into this style of life and succeed in love and marriage. If the social attitude of the child is one of anxious seeking to outdo his associates, sexuality will later be used as a means to this same end.

In the study and analysis of the individual patient, the main task is that of discovering his ' style of life ' and the peculiar goal of superiority which he has set himself as a child and which he still follows in some form or other. The individual's position in his family affords a general clue. His likes and dislikes, his ' heroes ' from history or fiction, his early and later choices of an occupation in life, all furnish clues. His manner of standing, walking, and sitting may reveal fundamental attitudes, and so may his way of shaking hands, and even the posture he assumes while asleep. ' When we see a person sleeping upon the back, stretched out like a soldier at attention, it is a sign that he wishes to appear as great as possible. One who lies curled up like a hedgehog with the sheet drawn over his head is not likely to be a striving or courageous character. . . . A person who sleeps on his stomach betrays stubbornness and negativity.' [1] The style of life comes out everywhere—though one may imagine that such easy analogies would often lead the analyst astray. In practice, the ' individual psychologist ' doubtless bases his conclusions on a comprehensive view of many behaviour traits. Thus, being the oldest child is not by itself a decisive fact. Each family is a case in itself. . . . There is no position in the family constellation which is favourable under all circumstances, no position . . . which must inexorably bring unfavourable development in its wake.' [2]

Dream analysis is used by Adler in much the same way as by Freud, except that he does not regard the dream as

---

[1] A. Adler, *op. cit.*, p. 215.

[2] E. Wexberg, *Individual Psychology*, translated by W. B. Wolfe (Cosmopolitan Book Corporation, 1929), p. 199.

essentially a fulfilment of old wishes. He thinks that it relates to the future rather than to the past. It is a sort of rehearsal of some important action that has soon to be performed in reality. Its importance to the psychologist is that it reveals the individual's style of life as applied to the approaching crisis. A hesitant man, on the verge of marriage, dreams of being *halted* at the boundary between two countries with a threat of imprisonment. The dream deals with the unsettled problems of the waking life and gravitates inevitably into the individual's fundamental attitude toward such problems, the attitude which was established in childhood and which has remained a fixed individual characteristic.

The maladjusted individual is to be treated by leading him gently to see his inferiority complex and his ingrained way of attaining superiority, so that he sees clearly what he is trying to do and what he is fearing and avoiding. While the individual's fundamental style of life cannot be changed after early childhood, it can be led into more practical and social forms.

Considered as a system or theory, Adler's psychology is certainly coherent. It appears too simple to be called depth psychology. The unconscious plays a comparatively small rôle, and is not regarded as separate from the conscious life. The style of life becomes so much a matter of course with the individual, and is so little understood, that we may well call it unconscious, but it becomes conscious in proportion as it is understood. Freud's two prime facts, resistance and transference, are encountered also by Adler and his school in their treatment of neurotic persons, but are interpreted in an un-Freudian way. The resistance is seen not as an unconscious opposition to the emergence of old repressed wishes, but as a defence against the treatment itself—the patient dreads being cured because if cured he would undertake tasks in which he might fail !

12

Similarly with transference—if the patient falls in love with the doctor, it is not real love, but just one way of getting the better of him. In general, the conscious and the unconscious are not two separate entities or antagonistic halves of the individual, but are bound together as having the same desires and trends. The unconscious inferiority complex and the conscious striving for power constitute a dynamic unity. We need no hypothetical ' warring entities,' as Adler puts the matter.

If you recall the phrase in which we embodied what we thought we had found to be Freud's three basal assumptions —' polarized wishful entities '—we see that Adler has rejected two of the three. He gets along without entities and without any ultimate polarity. He is still a motivationist, as much so as Freud, and fully accepts the principle of ' psychical causation.' The psychical causes which he finds are different from Freud's, but feeling of inferiority and goal of superiority are certainly psychological rather than physiological concepts. In their emphasis on childhood as the formative period Freud and Adler are in agreement, in spite of their disagreement as to what it is that happens in childhood that is so important for later life.

However true and adequate Adler's psychology may or may not be in the ultimate sense, it certainly embodies much proximate truth that is immediately applicable to life. One might say that his conceptions are easier than Freud's, easier to grasp and easier to apply. Especially in assisting children to master their problems, Adler's line of approach has proved its value, so that he has already won a position of influence in the educational field.

JUNG'S ' ANALYTIC PSYCHOLOGY '

C. G. Jung of Zurich (born 1875) came to know Freud personally after several years of study and practice of psycho-analysis, and for a few years the two men were closely associated, in [congresses and through correspondence. Freud thought so highly of this able young recruit that he made him president of the newly formed international association of psycho-analysis, believing, though no doubt mistakenly, that the public and scientific reception of the new movement would be more favourable if he himself remained in the background. But it soon became evident that Jung regarded Freud's conceptions as valuable and revolutionary, indeed, but as one-sided and somewhat immature; and he proceeded to expound the more complete doctrine, which he calls 'Analytical Psychology.'

Jung's improvements concerned the neuroses and the libido. With regard to the first, Freud, by tracing the origin of the adult's neurosis back to the Oedipus complex of the child, had shown the ' predisposing cause ' of the disease, but he had taken little account of the ' exciting cause.' An individual may carry around within him bad complexes left over from poor adaptations in childhood, and yet not fall victim to a neurosis until he encounters some difficult problem of life. The exciting cause of the neurosis is some situation which demands of the individual a fresh adaptation. He attempts to meet this new situation, but has not sufficient force. He fails in his new adjustment, and relapses or regresses into earlier habits of meeting difficult situations. He regresses to the line he took as an infant in adjusting himself to the family situation. His childish adjustment may have been poor, and reviving it now does not help him. As a child he may have taken refuge in phantasies, and now he regresses to that imaginary sort of solution of his problem. All this regression leads him away from his actual problem and its solution. If the present problem chances to solve itself, his infantile behaviour immediately disappears ; therefore the present difficulty of adjustment is the real cause of the neurosis.

Take away the obstacle in the path of life and this whole system of infantile phantasies at once breaks down and becomes again as inactive and ineffective as before. But do not let us forget that, to a certain extent, it is at work influencing us always and everywhere. . . . Therefore I no longer find the cause of the neurosis in the past, but in the present. I ask, what is the necessary task which the patient will not accomplish?[1]

In treating the neuroses, Jung adheres to Freud's technique of free association and dream analysis. He starts, however, with a study of the patient's present problem, and seeks to discover the elements of weakness in his attack upon it. The patient's dreams he interprets not simply as revealing old repressed sex wishes, such as the Oedipus complex, but as indicating the patient's unconscious attitude toward his present problem. By the analysis, the patient becomes conscious of his primitive attack on the problem, and is enabled to integrate the unconscious with the conscious. The analysis thus gives the patient an understanding of his present state as well as of his infantile past, and sends him out a better integrated personality. Freud objected to this moralizing tendency of Jung's work.

As to the libido, Jung gave it a broader meaning than even Freud, but in so doing he denied that it was distinctively sexual. He sought to include in it both Freud's libido and Adler's striving for superiority or will for power. Jung, the monistic harmonizer, regarded the primary libido as a general urge, equivalent to Schopenhauer's will to live or to Bergson's *élan vital*. It is the total vital

[1] C. G. Jung, *Collected Papers on Analytical Psychology*, translated by C. E. Long (Baillière, Tindall & Cox, 2nd edition, 1920), p. 232. The particular paper from which the quotation is made dates from 913.

energy seeking the goal of growth as well as of activity and reproduction. In the infant, it first finds an outlet in nutritive activities. The child's pleasure in gaining nourishment arises from the libido, but is not to be called in any sense sexual pleasure, since the sex urge has not yet differentiated itself from the primal urge to live. Jung has expressed himself forcibly enough regarding Freud's conception of infantile sexuality : [1]

A strictly Freudian analysis . . . is exclusively a sex-analysis, based upon the dogma that the relation of mother and child is necessarily sexual. Of course any Freudian will assure you that he does not mean coarse sexuality, but ' psycho-sexuality '—an unscientific and logically unjustifiable extension. . . . A child's regressive tendency can be designated an ' incestuous craving for the mother ' only figuratively. . . . So too with the term ' Oedipus complex ' : this is merely figurative. . . . The word ' incest ' has a definite meaning. . . . To apply the same term to a child's difficulties . . . is worse than absurd.

Freud has expressed himself with equal candour regarding Jung's purifying of the libido by removing its sexual atmosphere. In Jung's view, Freud was one-sided in his emphasis on sexuality, while as Freud saw the matter Jung was sacrificing the great gains that Freud himself had achieved in sex psychology.

Jung sought to aline his concept of the libido with the concept of energy in physics. Energy is transformed but remains the same energy, whether as heat, electricity, or movement of masses. So it is one psychical energy, one libido, that manifests itself now in self-assertion and again in sex desire. Freud had recognized one of these forms of energy and Adler the other, and each had one-sidedly tried to regard all energy as of one form. If energy is redirected

[1] C. G. Jung, *Contributions to Analytical Psychology*, translated by. H. G. and C. F. Baynes (Harcourt, Brace & Co., 1928), pp. 339, 340.

out of sex activity into art or some other sublimation, it is transformed and no longer remains sex desire, in the main, though some traces of the immediate source of the energy may remain in the sublimated activity.

Another important side of Jung's energy theory is that energy can be thought of as tending toward an end-state of equilibrium. Freud had always gone to the past of the individual for an understanding of present behaviour, and while Adler had spoken of goals, he also had gone back to infancy to find the goals which the individual had adopted as a result of his infantile situation. Both have imitated the 'causal-mechanical' type of explanation that is common in physical science. We find in physics the energy conception, which has never been harmonized with the causal-mechanical conception, and which seems even to be theoretically inconsistent with it ; but the energy conception is more in line with modern tendencies in physics, especially because it is quantitative. In psychology, to be sure, we cannot proceed in a strictly quantitative manner, but we are interested, at least in abnormal psychology, in values which are roughly quantitative, as one value is greater than another. Hence the energy conception is more adequate in analytical psychology than the causal-mechanical explanation of behaviour. A neurosis is a present attempt at adjustment to life, a poor attempt indeed, but at least an attempt at transformation and a new synthesis. The neurosis is to be cured, then, by the analyst's helping along this new synthesis, rather than by his merely unearthing past causes, though the latter procedure is of use as a preliminary stage in the treatment.

My condensed paraphrase of Jung's extensive discussions of this topic [1] is of course inadequate and may fail to

[1] See, for example, C. G. Jung, *Collected Papers on Analytical Psychology*, translated by C. E. Long, 2nd edition, 1920, pp. 396, 401, 417 ; and *Contributions to Analytical Psychology*, translated by H. G. and C. F. Baynes, 1928, pp. 1–70.

convey the author's idea. I should like to suggest for your consideration that there is some analogy between Jung's energic conception of a neurosis or of any adjustment as a fresh synthesis, on the one hand, and on the other the Gestalt conception of insight as ' closing a gap ' and reaching an equilibrium.

The differences between our three great psychopathologists can be brought out by reverting for a moment to the matter of dream interpretation. Jung has contrasted his own and the Freudian interpretations in the instance of a dream of a young man, recently graduated from the university, who had been unable to settle on an occupation and had fallen into a neurosis. The dream was : [1]

I was going up a flight of stairs with my mother and sister. When we reached the top I was told that my sister was soon to have a child.

This would be easy for a Freudian, climbing stairs being accepted as a regular symbol for sex activity, and the mother and sister being the regular objects of the infantile incest desires. The dream would be clearly a fulfilment of a repressed infantile wish. Not satisfied with this ready interpretation, Jung proceeded to obtain free associations starting from each element of the dream. The mother suggested neglect of his duties, since he had long neglected his mother. The sister suggested true love for a woman. Climbing the stairs suggested making a success of life, and the prospective baby suggested new birth or regeneration for himself. Jung concluded that the dream revealed the stirring of unconscious energies toward meeting the young man's present situation. How Adler would interpret this dream we cannot tell, lacking information as to whether the dreamer were the oldest child or younger than his sister, but since the dreamer did not climb his stairs alone, it looks as if his style of life was one of de-

[1] Jung, *Collected Papers*, etc., p. 219.

pendence on the support of other people. The fact that several divergent interpretations can be made of the same dream, each one of them useful in the hands of the analyst, makes one stop and think. One wonders how many different dramas have been built upon the life of Napoleon, good interpretations in their several ways, but none of them, certainly, conveying Napoleon's life. No interpretation really conveys the dream. Speaking for myself, I have grave doubts of the validity of any dream interpretation. What underlies a given dream is certainly much more than finds a place in any interpretation. Fortunately, the object in view in interpreting a dream is not to understand that particular dream, but to discover some complex, or wish, or aspiration, or style of life, of the person who has the dream. If we find out something genuine regarding him, our practical aim is met even if we have grossly misinterpreted the dream itself. Scientifically, however, if not practically, the distinction is worth bearing in mind.

JUNG'S INTROVERSION AND EXTROVERSION

Far from belittling the work of Freud and of Adler, Jung was much concerned to incorporate the achievements of both into his own system. But how to harmonize or synthesize doctrines so radically divergent the one from the other ? Freud regarded a dream or a neurosis as motivated by repressed sex desires, Adler by the will for power. Each motive alone appears adequate, but the two are irreconcilable. Jung solved the enigma by his famous doctrine of psychological types. One person may be motivated in the Freudian way, another in the Adlerian way. The one who is motivated by the will for power, Jung argued, must have his interests focused on the self, while the one who is sex-motivated must focus his interests on the love-object. Generalizing, Jung believed it possible to distinguish two types of individual, one whose interest and attention centred by preference within himself, and the other whose interest and attention went out to the social and physical environment. The *introvert* was turned inward, the *extrovert* (or *extravert*) was turned outward. The extrovert, motivated by Freud's libido, was dominated by feeling; the introvert, motivated by Adler's will for power, was dominated by thought and inclined to reverie and rumination. Using his own conception of libido as life energy, Jung could say that in extroversion the libido moved outward toward objects, and in introversion inward toward the individual himself.

None of Jung's theories has aroused so much general interest as this of introversion and extroversion. It is a fascinating task to classify people and find some of them belonging to one type and some to another. The ancients used to classify men under the four temperaments, sanguine, choleric, phlegmatic, and melancholic. Following Galton's studies of mental imagery, toward the close of the last century, psychologists liked to classify people as visual, auditory, or motor in type, with a few scattered ones belonging to the olfactory and other types; and it was suggested that such classification was important in education, for if a child belonged to the auditory type, visual instruction would fail to reach him. So children were tested for imagery, but immediately the surprising result appeared that they all belonged to the mixed type. Such a result is always found wherever we are able to measure a trait. We find individuals not falling into separate groups, but all distributed about a single mean or average, with those near to the mean most frequent and a gradual tapering off toward the extremes.

Such facts have driven psychologists to scepticism regarding types of people. Accordingly, we are inclined to be sceptical of the introvert and extrovert types, if the implication is that mankind fall into these two groups. However, Jung recognized this difficulty in a measure, and spoke also of the ' ambivert ' whose libido went both outward and inward and whose interests were not predominantly either in the self or in the object. Psychologists have taken up Jung's conception of types, and have sought tests for locating an individual on a scale extending from extreme introversion to extreme extroversion ; and it is found possible to do this, though with the understanding that most individuals fall toward the middle of the scale.

The way in which psychologists have gone to work to measure people on the introversion-extroversion scale consists in amassing as many different symptoms or indications of introversion or extroversion as possible, and then counting up the symptoms of each sort that an individual displays or recognizes as his own. He is asked such questions as the following :

> Do you like to be by yourself a great deal ?
> Do you confide in others ?
> Do you like to speak in public ?
> Do you wish to be always calm and collected ?
> Do you like monotonous work ?
> Do you think a great deal before reaching a decision ?
> Do you like to indulge in reverie ?
> Do you keep a personal diary ?
> Do you prefer to read of adventures or to have them ?

You can perhaps decide for yourselves what answer to each of these questions is the introvert answer, though sometimes it is not perfectly obvious. In my own opinion, indeed, there are at least two variables lumped together in the introvert-extrovert scale as at present used, and in Jung's original formulation as well. One variable would be the tendency to immediate overt action as opposed to the tendency to deliberate, ruminate, and perhaps daydream. The other variable would be the interest in other people and in social activity. The two variables seem to me probably independent of each other. For example, I am sure we could find people who were prone to daydream and ruminate and who at the same time were much interested in social activity. Also it is interesting to learn that scientific observers, inventors, and mechanics are usually held to tend toward introversion, though they are certainly absorbed in objects. There may be more than two independent variables mixed together in the distinction between introverts and extroverts.

Jung has elaborated his type theory in several directions.[1] He recognizes another basis of cleavage, according to which individuals can be assigned to a sensing type, a thinking type, a feeling type, and an intuitive type. Most interesting, perhaps, is his suggestion that persons who are extroverted in their conscious lives are introverted in the unconscious, and vice versa. ' In the case of an introvert, for example, there exists alongside, or rather behind his conscious attitude, an unconscious extroverted attitude which automatically compensates his conscious one-sidedness. . . . The unconscious, so far as we can now see, has a compensatory function in respect to consciousness.'[2]

THE UNCONSCIOUS AS VIEWED BY JUNG AND OTHERS

The unconscious is as significant a concept to Jung as to Freud. If anything, Jung makes more of it. He distinguished between the personal and the collective or racial unconscious. The personal unconscious is formed in part by repression from the conscious, as Freud had pointed out; but it also includes, according to Jung, other experiences and knowledge that have been forgotten or

[1] See his *Psychological Types*, translated by H. G. Baynes (Routledge, 1923).

[2] C. G. Jung, *Contributions to Analytical Psychology*, 1928, pp. 306-7.

dissociated out of consciousness and still other material that has been acquired unconsciously. More fundamental is the collective unconscious, out of which both the conscious and the unconscious life of the individual develop. Only rarely does this deepest unconscious show itself in dreams or in the neuroses, but the phantasies of really insane persons sometimes bring to the surface weird ideas and ways of thought that seem like vestiges of the primitive thinking of the race.

The collective or racial unconscious is inherited. It is inherited, as everything else is, by way of the structure of the organism. Inherited brain structure disposes the individual to think and act as the race has been habituated to think and act through countless generations of primitive life. The collective unconscious may be said to consist of instincts and 'primordial ideas' or 'archetypes.' The instincts are primitive ways of acting, and the archetypes are primitive ways of thinking, but the two cannot be completely separated, for thinking and acting go together, especially in primitive forms of life.

The theory of archetypes or primordial ideas is not to be confused with the long-abandoned theory of innate ideas. The collective unconscious does not contain ideas exactly— nothing so clean-cut as that. But it contains natural ways of thinking, lines of least resistance, tendencies to gravitate in our ideas toward primitive modes of thought. In dreams, in the night terrors of children, in the hallucinations and delusions of the insane, and even in waking life when we are caught off our guard by something for which we are totally unprepared, such as an earthquake, our recently won scientific conceptions of natural processes drop away from us, and we think animistically or have vague primitive notions of sympathetic magic and of spirits, fairies, witches, dragons, and devils. Father, mother, and child, male and female, generation, growth and decay, are primitive facts which have so impressed themselves on racial thought that they constantly reappear as symbols in the thought of to-day. We gravitate toward them as easy and explanatory ideas, and speak of the ' birth of a nation ' or the ' decay of an institution,' scarcely noticing the figure of speech. Some archetypes, such as that of energy, have been appropriated by scientific thought ; and it may often be of advantage to an individual's mental health to become aware of some of his racial archetypes, as of some of his instincts, and to integrate them with his conscious thought and action. The study of mythology and of primitive customs is valuable to analytical psychology for the light it throws on the collective unconscious.

Some of Jung's statements regarding the unconscious are surprising, to say the least, and seem to imply some other concept of the unconscious than the one we have been setting forth. What shall we make of passages like the following ? [1]

The conscious consists only of those ideational complexes that are directly associated with the ego. . . . In the early years of life there is in the first place scarcely any conscious, although very early the existence of psychic processes is evident. But these processes are not focused in an organized ego ; they have no centrum, and therefore no continuity, without which a conscious personality is impossible. . . . Only when the child begins to say ' I ' is there a perceptible continuity of consciousness. . . .

Now if we were to ask what would happen if there were no schools, and children were left entirely to themselves, we should have to answer that children would to a great extent remain unconscious. . . .

The child develops out of an originally unconscious and animal-like condition to consciousness ; first to a primitive, and then slowly to a civilized consciousness. The condition in the first two or three years of his life, when the child is unconscious of himself, can be compared to the animal state.

[1] C. G. Jung, *Contributions to Analytical Psychology*, 1928, p. 315.

It is surprising to be told that the child is unconscious till he begins to speak of himself as ' I.' That is dating consciousness later than Watson did, when he identified it with ' verbalization ' and accordingly denied it to children who had not yet learned to talk. If the child of a few months of age, or of two years, is ' unconscious,' it cannot be in the same sense in which a chloroformed patient is unconscious.

' Unconscious ' shares the varied usage of ' conscious,' which may mean ' conscious of an object,' or ' self-conscious,' or simply ' conscious ' or awake. Titchener, though such an ardent introspectionist, abandoned the use of ' consciousness ' because he found it could not be limited to one definite meaning. One common use of ' unconscious,' which is perhaps near to that of Jung in the quotation, refers to the lack of insight or lack of premeditation that characterizes much of every one's activity. We call a performance unconscious if it has not been analysed by the performer. He may not have analysed the motives behind his action nor its consequences. So he may be unconsciously injuring some one, and he may unconsciously be trying to injure some one. He may consciously be trying to help some one, but helping a person may be a way of demonstrating that person's inferiority. Motives come in compounds often difficult to analyse, and the separate motives analysed out of an act by Jung or Freud or Adler are therefore unconscious in this sense to the performer of the act. The child would act unconsciously in this sense, though perhaps no more so than the adult. Something of this sort must be Jung's meaning, though he might be better satisfied if we paraphrased him by saying that the child at first reacts impulsively or instinctively to the environment and only gradually becomes a relatively independent unit. Jung goes on to say that the unconscious state of the young child is a 'state of complete fusion with the surrounding conditions,' and that the ' psyche of early infancy is to a large degree a part of the maternal psyche, and soon too . . . a part of the paternal psyche.' What these expressions mean in practice is that nervous troubles and behaviour difficulties in the young child are symptoms of maladjustment to life on the part of the parents, who are the ones to be analysed and treated if the child is to be helped.

To the psychopathologist, the unconscious is by no means an academic concept or a mere scientific hypothesis to be submitted to test. It is a tool that they feel they could not dispense with. Janet, Prince, Freud, Adler, Jung, and many others all gravitate toward it and all define it differently. What real use do they have for it ? As explained by MacCurdy,[1] they need it so as to be able to stick to psychological terms even when going beyond the narrow confines of consciousness. Why not admit that all processes going on outside of consciousness are purely physiological, and speak of them in physiological terms ? Well, try it once. Speak of an unconscious motive in physiological terms. You can do so only in the vaguest way, however well you know physiology, and if you took your task of physiological description seriously you would be forced to speak in terms of the neurones and of very minute and detailed processes. You could not repeat all this detail whenever you wanted to refer to the matter again, and so you would be practically forced back to your psychological term, unconscious motive. The same would be true of unconscious thinking, etc. To describe behaviour in behaviour terms does not prevent any one who can from describing it in physiological terms. All psychological processes are at the same time physiological processes ; it is just a question of which set of descriptive terms you are going to apply to them.

[1] J. T. MacCurdy, *Mental Hygiene*, 1921, vol. v. pp. 236–65.

We might tarry longer with the unconscious ; and we might tarry indefinitely with the psychopathologists, but we may as well come to a halt, and permit ourselves just one closing reflection. Besides the definite adherents of Freud, of Adler, and of Jung, there are very many psychiatrists who do not join any one school, and who see nothing amiss in adopting methods and theories from all and so constructing each one a system for himself. Forty years of emphasis by a few psychopathologists on the mental factors in a neurosis have made an impression on the general body of psychiatrists, so that the psychogenic idea of the neuroses is very widely held to-day, and even in regard to such psychoses as dementia præcox and manic-depressive insanity there is much present inclination to stress mental factors. Thus Freud and Janet and the rest in their different ways have contributed toward the strengthening of the ' psychic ' type of psychiatry as against the ' somatic ' ; and this whole development has been of immense interest to psychology as well. The clinical psychologist, like the psychiatrist, looks at the numerous concepts of psycho-analysis, analytical psychology, and individual psychology from the pragmatic point of view, and is pleased if any of them work well in the treatment of problem children. The academic psychologist, being also somewhat of a pragmatist in his own field, asks whether such a concept as the id, in which Freud seems to have made room for Jung's collective unconscious, can play a useful rôle as a scientific theory. For the present, the academic psychologist has a vision of these attractive theories and conceptions surrounded each one by a halo which on closer observation takes the form of a question mark.

CHAPTER VI

PURPOSIVISM OR HORMIC PSYCHOLOGY

JUST as existentialism sees in sensation the fundamental fact of psychology, as behaviourism sees
it in bodily movement, and the Gestalt psychology
in perception of patterns, so there is a psychology that
takes its start from the fact of purpose. Human activity
shows these various aspects, if not more besides, and it is
not strange that one or another should excite the special
interest of a psychologist and lead him to build a psychological system upon the particular phase of activity
which strikes him as the most significant.

THE FACT OF PURPOSE

The fact of human purpose cannot be disputed. Those
psychologists who rule it out from psychology are themselves very purposeful individuals. No one can read
Titchener without realizing that he is in the hands of a
man of purpose. He wishes to eliminate purpose, meaning,
and value, because only so, he believes, can psychology
get down to a matter-of-fact description. In concluding
his prolegomena, he indicates what the immediate purpose
of existential psychology must be in handling the data
that are available : ' We do not even aim at imprinting
a new pattern upon the data of psychology . . . we only
hope to weave them all consistently into a pattern already
in part designed.' Certainly, Watson is a purposeful
individual, though he has no use for purpose in his psychol-

13

ogy : ' In 1912 the behaviourists decided either to give up psychology or else to make it a natural science. . . . The interest of the behaviourist in man's doings is more than the interest of the spectator—he wants to control man's reactions.' I am not quoting these authors to convict them of inconsistency. They are permitting themselves in these passages to talk as human beings and not as psychologists. They are talking about psychology, not talking psychology. But one may cite them as well as anybody else to point out the common sense fact or prima facie fact of purpose. Whether this fact is to be explained away or made a fundamental fact of psychology is another question.

Professor Z. Y. Kuo of Fuh Tan University, China, an adherent of the American behaviouristic group, believes that behaviourism has as yet gone only half-way in freeing itself from the mentalistic ideas of traditional psychology. What he says about purpose is worth quoting as a forcible statement of the ultra-negative attitude toward any use of this concept in psychology.[1]

The concept of purpose is a lazy substitute for . . . careful and detailed analysis. . . . With better understanding of the . . . elementary stimuli and the stimulus pattern, with more knowledge of physiological facts, and with clearer insight into the behaviour history, the concept of purpose of whatever form will eventually disappear. . . . The duty of a behaviourist is to describe behaviour in exactly the same way as the physicist describes the movement of a machine. . . . This human machine behaves in a certain way because environmental stimulation has forced him to do so. . . .

The rejection of the concept of purpose implies a repudiation of the current view of trial and error learning in animals. For this view is based on the notion that . . . the animal

---

[1] Z. Y. Kuo, ' The Fundamental Error of the Concept of Purpose and the Trial and Error Fallacy,' *Psychological Review*, 1928, vol. xxxv. pp. 414-33.

has a purpose, or is making some effort to solve a problem. . . .
If we accept the view that every movement of the animal is
passive and forced by environmental stimuli . . . certainly
this concept of trial and error must be abandoned. . . .
The purpose is preconceived or created by the experimenter
—the animal itself has no aim or goal. . . . Whether an act
is successful or unsuccessful depends on the purpose of the
experimenter. From the objective standpoint, one act is just
as successful or just as unsuccessful as any other one.

Certainly, Kuo writes like a purposeful individual, and
he even admits that an experimenter can have a purpose.
But the animal experimented on can have no purpose,
neither can a human being who is studied by the psychologist. In other words, purpose can be allowed to remain
in our common sense world, but must be eliminated from
the field of psychological study. The reasons urged for its
elimination are that it is a mentalistic and not an objective
concept, and that it is crude and unanalysed and should
give place to a more detailed and physiological description.

Purpose, then, presents itself as a fact, and the question
is how to deal with it. We may refuse to have anything
to do with it, we may cut it up and save the pieces, we
may admit it to the society of psychological facts and try
to find a place for it, or we may make it king of psychology
and subordinate all our other facts to it. If we take the
last course we are purposivists.

Purpose, as we commonly use the term, implies two
facts that do not always go together. It implies foresight
of the outcome of a certain action, and it implies desire for
that outcome. The aviator in a certain predicament
may foresee that he is going to strike a tree, but such is not
exactly his purpose. The hungry infant cries and slashes
about, without necessarily having any foresight of the
replete condition toward which it is striving. Purposivism
means the primacy of striving or seeking, rather than the

primacy of foresight. Sometimes the broader word, *horme* (hor-may, a Greek word meaning urge), is substituted for purpose, and purposivism rechristened the hormic psychology.

McDougall's Promulgation of Purposivism

In a broad sense, hormic psychology evidently covers the systems of Freud, Adler, and Jung, and possibly even the Gestalt psychology. But there is a school that centres its psychology so definitely about the fact of purpose that we can distinguish it as the purposivistic school. The chief spokesman of this school is William McDougall (born 1871), formerly at Cambridge, London, and Oxford, and more recently at Harvard and Duke Universities. McDougall's hormic psychology took shape in 1908, and is thus the oldest of the schools that we are considering, with the exception of existentialism and of Freud's psycho-analysis. McDougall was probably not influenced by Freud at the outset, since he was interested at the time in a social psychology rather than in an abnormal psychology. More recently he has hailed Freud as a pioneer in hormic psychology, while adhering himself to a system that is very different from that of Freud.

After early work of much importance on experimental and physiological psychology, McDougall undertook in 1908 to provide a psychological foundation for the social sciences. His *Introduction to Social Psychology* is a work of outstanding importance in the history of our period. Before that time psychology had made no serious attempt to be of service to the social sciences, but had left it to each sociologist or historian or economist to improvise a psychology for his own use. That these improvised psychologies were crude was really the fault of the scientific psychologists who had taken no pains to consider how they themselves could provide a psychology that should throw light on social problems. Scientific psychology had been so immersed in the study of intellectual performances, and in the details of sensation, memory, and habit formation that it had scarcely touched the problems of motivation. Now the social sciences were not concerned with the details of mental or motor processes, but they would like to know the motives of human conduct. Did men live in groups and submit to government through fear of each other, or through calculation of the greatest good to the greatest number, or simply through inertia and imitation ? Was religion the working out of a religious instinct, and politics the working out of a political instinct ? Was conscience a native faculty for distinguishing right from wrong ? Those who needed an answer to these questions took the best answer that suggested itself, while psychology passed by on the other side.

McDougall's revolt against the established order was thus twofold. He objected to the rough and ready psychology that he found in the social sciences, and he objected to the one-sided intellectualism of psychology as it was. He objected to the dogma that introspection was the one true method of psychology, ' for the life of emotion and the play of motives is the part of our mental life which offers the least advantageous field for introspective observation and description.' Non-introspective studies of animals, children, and abnormal adults held the most promise for the study of motivation. The intellectualizing tendency of psychology had led to the assumption that all human conduct was rational and dependent upon foresight of consequences. But why should certain consequences be more desirable than others unless there were some primary desires, needs, or impulses ? Just as in geometry we have to base our reasonings upon axioms which we cannot prove, so conduct goes back ultimately to primary impulses that are irrational just because they are ultimate and self-evident to the individual.

It is the mental forces, the sources of energy, which set the ends and sustain the course of all human activity—of which forces the intellectual processes are but the servants, instruments, or means—that must be clearly defined, and whose history in the race and in the individual must be made clear, before the social sciences can build upon a firm psychological foundation. Now . . . psychologists . . . have generally neglected these socially more important problems.[1]

Though McDougall's emphasis on instincts was new, he did find valuable antecedents in the discussions of human instincts by Darwin, G. H. Schneider, and William James. James had written : [2]

Nothing is commoner than the remark that Man differs from lower creatures by the almost total lack of instincts, and the assumption of their work in him by ' reason '. . . .We must of course avoid a quarrel about words, and the facts of the case are really tolerably plain. Man has a far greater variety of *impulses* than any lower animal ; and any one of these impulses, taken in itself, is as ' blind ' as the lowest instinct can be ; but, owing to man's memory, power of reflection, and power of inference, they come each one to be felt by him, after he has . . . experienced their results, in connection with a *foresight* of those results.

McDougall set to work in earnest to develop a psychology of the motivation of human conduct. As the primary motives he took the ' instincts ' of man. He did not fix his attention exclusively on instinctive movements, and did not at all accept Herbert Spencer's conception of an instinct as a chain of reflexes. An instinct for McDougall was not a mere mechanical sensorimotor performance.

[1] W. McDougall, *Introduction to Social Psychology* (Methuen & Co., 1908 ; J. W. Luce & Co., 1909), pp. 3, 4.
[2] W. James, *Principles of Psychology*, 1890, vol. ii. pp. 389, 390.

He noticed that common sense often linked an instinct with an emotion. Fear, for example, can be spoken of as an instinct or as an emotion, and so can curiosity and others. It seemed to him in typical cases that the core of an instinct was the emotion. Hardly distinguished from the emotion, by common sense, is a conative or striving element, the impulse toward a certain goal. Thus fear includes an impulse to escape, and anger an impulse to damage the adversary. Instinct is then mental as well as motor ; and, further, on the sensory side it consists not in a mere passive reception of the stimulus but in a singling out of the exciting object, attending to it, perceiving it.

For McDougall, then, an instinct is a primary motive, a native spring of action. It is not simply an unlearned connexion between a certain stimulus and a certain movement. He analyses it into three main parts or phases :

1. On the receptive side, it is a predisposition to notice certain stimuli that arouse activity.

2. On the executive side, it is a predisposition to make certain movements or to produce certain changes in the situation.

3. Between the receptive and the executive sides is the emotion, the core of the whole instinct.

Thus, for example, the fear instinct or instinct of escape covers the fixing of attention upon suspicious objects, the emotion of fear and impulse to escape, and the varied movements by which this impulse is executed.

It may be well to include here McDougall's list of instincts, partly to show the difference between his type of hormic psychology and that of Freud, Jung, or Adler, who usually speak of two instincts or two groups of instincts. I will give the enlarged list presented by McDougall in his more recent *Outline of Psychology*, 1923.

The instinct to escape from danger, with the accompanying emotion of fear ;

The instinct of combat, with the emotion of anger ;

Repugnance and disgust ;

Parental instinct to protect the young, with tender feeling ;

Instinctive cry of distress, with feeling of helplessness ;

Mating or sex instinct, with sex emotion ;

Curiosity ;

Submission, with feeling of humility ;

Self-assertion, with feeling of superiority ;

Seeking company (herd instinct), with feeling of loneliness ;

Food-seeking, with appetite for food ;

Hoarding instinct, with feeling of ownership ;

Constructive instinct, with feeling of creativeness ;

Laughter, with feeling of amusement.

There are also minor instincts, such as those of sneezing and coughing, defecation and urination, which play no great rôle in social life though the feeling and impulse accompanying them are sometimes momentarily very strong. But the major instincts, McDougall holds, do play a great rôle and provide all the primary motives necessary to account for the family, for social grouping, and for war, religion, and all other social activities.

The instincts are not acquired by the individual but handed down to him by heredity. They are the original springs of all his activity. Without them, his intellectual and motor machinery would be like a factory with the power cut off. The human machine would be passive, driven simply by the stimuli that chanced to strike it. A reflex appears to be driven in this way by the stimulus of the moment. But what we call *behaviour* differs from an aggregation of reflexes. Behaviour shows the following characteristics : [1]

[1] W. McDougall, *Outline of Psychology* (Methuen & Co. Ltd.), pp. 43–6.

1. It shows some degree of spontaneity and independence of the environment, at the same time that it is responsive to the environment.

2. It shows persistence in a line of activity which may be started by a momentary stimulus but which continues after that stimulus has ceased. A rabbit scurrying to its hole after a momentary noise is an example.

3. With all the persistence there is much variation in the motor behaviour. If an obstacle is encountered, a detour is made and the same goal reached as if there had been no obstacle.

4. The varied activity comes to an end when a certain result is attained. The cat makes a dash for a tree and up the trunk and then sits down comfortably on a limb and watches the dog.

5. Often the first part of a behaviour series consists of movements that prepare the animal for the next stage. The stealthy crouching of a hunting cat is an example.

6. If the situation arousing a behaviour series is often repeated, the varied behaviour takes a more definite form, useless movements are eliminated, short-cuts and other improvements come in, and in a word the animal learns by the process of trial and error.

In short, behaviour, objectively considered, shows goal seeking ; and those behaviourists who shut their eyes to this fundamental characteristic cannot be called genuine students of behaviour. Goal seeking requires motives, and the primary motives are provided by the instincts.

Though McDougall thus insisted on inherited instincts as the fundamental motives, it would not be fair to say that he overlooked the importance of learning. An instinct, he proceeded to explain, was subject to modification through the animal's experience. The instinct for anger and combat, for example, is modified in two principal ways. On the sensory side it is modified by being attached to new stimuli, i.e. by becoming conditioned as Pavlov would say. Angry behaviour in an infant is aroused by physical restraint and by physical interference with the infant's movements. Later, restraint or interference of a more subtle sort, manifested by verbal commands or otherwise, will arouse anger. On the motor or executive side, also, much learning and modification occur. The slashing and kicking of the angry infant gives place to biting and scratching, to hair pulling and striking with the fist, and to verbal and other indirect ways of hurting the adversary.

Thus McDougall leaves much scope for learning both on the sensory and on the motor side, but he still holds that the core of the instinct, the emotion, remains practically the same in spite of all learning and experience. It is this emotional (and impulsive) core that gives continuity to the instinct. The infant reacting to some one holding his elbows by slashing and kicking, and the adult reacting to an offensive letter by setting on foot certain measures designed to injure the offender, appear on the surface to be performing very different acts, but what holds these different acts together under the same instinct is the angry emotion and impulse to hurt that are common to both.

Not only do instincts become modified in the ways described, but they also become combined into complex attitudes or sentiments. McDougall speaks of the instincts as being originally separate tendencies, which become combined in the course of the individual's experience. More than one instinct gets attached to the same person, object, or situation, and through this sort of combination the sentiments of the older child and adult are developed. Patriotism is such a sentiment. Patriotism is not an instinct nor a primary emotion. One's country becomes tied up with more than a single instinct, and the complex sentiment of patriotism is the result. The country in danger arouses fear; the country attacked by another country arouses anger; the country in rivalry with another arouses self-assertion; the country as our home arouses emotions of the loving variety. Our country is associated with several emotions and instincts, and our complex attitude of patriotism thus develops and becomes a driving force in our behaviour.

The child develops sentiments toward individuals such as his father and mother, and toward institutions such as school and church that arouse varying emotions in him. He develops a sentiment toward himself, the self-regarding sentiment, to which McDougall assigns great importance in self-control, morality, and achievement. This self-regarding sentiment is based chiefly on the two instincts of self-assertion and submission. One has by nature the will for power and also a balancing ability to recognize superiority in others and to submit more or less gracefully. Much learning goes into the development of the individual's attitude toward himself.

McDougall and others have exercised their ingenuity in tracing the probable instinctive sources of the complex sentiments and attitudes of adult life. He holds that it is these sentiments rather than the bare instincts that are the direct motivating factors in adult behaviour. He does not say, as he is sometimes supposed to say, that all human behaviour is driven directly by instincts. Rather, what he says is that behaviour is driven by sentiments built up out of the instincts, and still possessing the emotional and impulsive quality of the instincts. Behaviour is not driven by purely rational considerations, but by loves and hates, interests, zeals, rivalries, enthusiasms, all of which have an emotional and impulsive character derived originally from the instincts. Social behaviour is not based fundamentally on rational considerations, nor on a single social instinct, but on a combination of many or all of the instincts. The herd instinct, by itself, would simply keep men together in groups ; but, once they are grouped, all their other instincts become adjusted to social situations and become combined into sentiments which are the motive forces of all kinds of social activity.

Such was the type of psychology which McDougall presented to the world in 1908. It was received with enthusiasm by psychologists—by many though not all of them—and led to many discussions, books, and university courses on social psychology by psychologists. It created social psychology as a branch of psychology, where previously it had been treated almost exclusively by sociologists. It was received with great interest also by the students of social science, and seemed for a time to be just what they had been waiting for. Instincts as the basis of social institutions became the theme of a succession of books by sociologists and economists. Graham Wallas, the English economist, wrote on *Human Nature in Politics* (1908) and on *The Great Society* (1914), following McDougall in large measure, though he was not quite ready to concede that man's thinking was wholly driven by such instincts as McDougall had listed. Wallas clung to the view that there was an instinct of rationality, in the sense that man liked to think and appreciated rationality for its own sake and not simply if and when it led to the satisfaction of some other instinct. At any rate, Wallas accepted the instincts as inherent demands of the individual—demands which society had to meet if the individual were to be kept contented. Our present industrialized society, he feared, had got so far away from the primitive conditions of life to which the instincts were adapted, that it was no longer able to meet the instinctive demands of the individual. By mechanizing industry it allowed the workman little play for his self-assertion, and by delaying the age of marriage it thwarted the sex instinct. Thus the individual in our modern society was apt to have thwarted instincts, 'baulked dispositions,' and in consequence to be restless and neurotic. Society needed remodelling so as to afford proper scope for the instincts. This same line of thought was followed by a number of other influential writers,[1] and seemed to be very illuminating.

A Hot Debate on Instinct

McDougall's doctrine of instincts, though received with momentary enthusiasm, ran counter to what may be called the professional bias of the sociologists. With their eyes fixed on the social group as the important object of study, they were less impressed by the inherent demands of the individual than by another line of undoubted facts indicating that the individual was moulded by society. The individual derives his language, his beliefs, his manners, and customs from the social environment. Undoubtedly, there is much more that he derives from this source, exposed as he is from infancy, in the family, on the playground, and in school, to the influence of other people. All that the anthropologists call the culture of the group appears to be imposed upon the individual and not invented or demanded by him. While to the psychologist it may be self-evident that society is composed of individuals and must meet the demands of individuals, to the sociologist the main fact is that society is there before any given individual and proceeds from birth onward to form and standardize the individual into conformity with its own demands. Thus we behave alike, and we ' behave like human beings,' not in the main because of our instincts, but because of the culture that is received in turn by every one of us. Such is the characteristic view of the sociologist.

[1] For example, O. Tead, *Instincts in Industry* (Houghton Mifflin Co., 1918) ; C. Parker, *The Casual Labourer and Other Essays* (Harcourt, Brace & Co., 1920). The latter draws not only on McDougall's list of instincts, but on Freud's transference of emotion and on Adler's inferiority complex and compensation.

Among the sociologists, then, a long-smouldering discontent with the doctrine of instincts broke loose about 1920. The greatest single conflagration was a book by L. L. Bernard, in 1924, entitled *Instinct: A Study of Social Psychology*, and devoted to demonstrating the silliness of much current talk about instinct and the unimportance of instinct in society. One part of the author's task was easy enough. No two psychologists gave the same list of instincts. Some allowed over a hundred, while others by pruning and combining brought the number down to one or two. Such disagreement in details argued against the validity of the whole conception.

Bernard's more serious criticism was that what were called instincts, both in common speech and in the psychologies, were largely learned activities. Mating, parental care, self-assertion, acquisitiveness or constructiveness, as we see them among men, are complex systems of activities acquired by the individual through his contact with the social environment. They do not have the earmarks of inheritable units. To speak of a central ' core,' emotional in character, present in all the varied activities that are said to belong under an instinct, strikes Bernard as mystical or metaphysical. There are instincts, probably many of them, Bernard believes, but they are small, elementary acts, not at all like the inclusive activities that we commonly call instincts. The sociologist and the social reformer should not forget the existence of these little instincts, but need attach little importance to them. They do not play the rôle that McDougall assigned to the instincts ; they do not set the goals and furnish the energy of man's behaviour.

What does set the goals and supply the stimuli to activity is the environment, in Bernard's opinion, especially the social environment. The environment furnishes the formative factors which control the development of intelligence and of conduct. We must remember that man, in the course of many generations, has built around himself a highly artificial environment, both of material objects that he uses, and of customs and institutions by which the behaviour of each new arrival upon the scene is regulated. No doubt, these social arrangements have to take some heed of the individual's biological needs ; but in the main the individual is plastic and is moulded by environmental pressures.

A few sentences from Bernard will illustrate his point of view.[1]

There are two well-defined viewpoints in the social sciences regarding the importance of a theory of the instincts as a basis for the development of social theory. One group of writers and teachers contend that the instincts are of secondary importance in the motivation of social conduct. . . . They maintain that whatever instincts man possesses are too elementary and too decidedly biological in character to be primarily determinative of his social adjustments. . . . Civilized man, they hold, is a cultivated animal living in an artificial construction, society. This artificial organization, human society, is constantly becoming more artificial and derivative, even to the extent of suppressing in large measure the native impulses of man. . . . Under the artificial or civilized régime he selects other objects for expenditure of effort than those which would be dictated solely by his native impulses or instincts, if they were allowed to control his conduct.

Those supporting the opposing view contend that man is still the creature of instinct, although he has learned for the most part to guide his instinctive impulses into more efficient and socialized channels in keeping with the expanded needs of civilization. . . . The instinctivists, fairly represented by McDougall, maintain that the acquired elements in character or control are formed under the dominance of the instincts.

---

[1] L. L. Bernard, *Instinct*, etc. (Allen & Unwin, 1924), pp. 26, 27, 54.

The environmentalists maintain the opposite and look to the environment, especially to the psycho-social environment, for the formative factors.

Bernard counts himself decidedly as an environmentalist. For the most part, he speaks of environmental pressures as determining the individual's behaviour. He admits that the individual is not exactly putty, and that environmental pressures are really stimuli that arouse the individual's responses. He would appear to stand on much the same ground as Kuo, who said, you will remember, that the ' human machine behaves in a certain way because environment stimulation has forced him to do so,' only that Bernard is particularly concerned to stress the social environment. He appears to have little more use for purposes or motives than Kuo has. But you will find Bernard lapsing occasionally into a way of speaking that seems to give away his whole case. Notice what he says under the head of ' Environmental Dominance ' : [1]

Civilization is itself in large part a system of sublimations and repressions. We do not give our pugnacious, sexual, gustatory, fear, and gregarious impulses free rein. On the contrary we build up innumerable controls over them in order that we may not destroy the fabric of culture by a ' return to nature ' through a blind following of our impulses. . . . The best method of control . . . is by what we call sublimation. This involves the turning of the impulses into derivative and substitute channels. . . . Our formative institutions . . . are always busy with this problem of the most effective control systems and gradually . . . should be able to devise a system which will bend the native impulses to the service of the best abstract ideals of a cultural civilization. Thus environment, rather than instinct, now shapes our behaviour in the main. Environment even utilizes instinct in the service of its own . . . ideals.

---

[1] L. L. Bernard, *An Introduction to Social Psychology* (Allen & Unwin, 1926), pp. 138, 139.

If this last quotation fairly represents Bernard's point of view, I must say I see no fundamental difference between him and McDougall. McDougall, to be sure, takes the standpoint of the individual and his demands upon society, while Bernard takes that of the social organizer or reformer who wishes to utilize these demands for the advantage of society. But both are speaking of native impulses which can be redirected or find new outlets. McDougall attempts to show in some detail how the instincts work out in social life. He writes, for example : [1]

The instinct of pugnacity has played a part second to none in the evolution of social organization, and in the present age it operates more powerfully than any other in producing demonstrations of collective emotion and action on a great scale. . . . But its modes of expression have changed with the growth of civilization ; as the development of law and custom discourages and renders unnecessary the bodily combat of individuals, this gives place to the collective combat of communities and to the more refined forms of combat within communities.

Bernard might have quoted this passage to illustrate what he meant by ' control by sublimation.' It is no doubt true that McDougall thinks of this process as more important in social behaviour than Bernard does. Bernard thinks of behaviour as a system of habits formed out of the random movements or ' little instincts ' of infancy by a process of conditioning under the pressure of the environment; so that in the main the behaviour of the adult should have no connexion with the ' native impulses.'

The sociologists were very ready to throw off their adherence to the doctrine of instincts. I have distorted the course of events somewhat by placing their revolt

[1] W. McDougall, *An Introduction to Social Psychology*, 1908, p. 279.

14

against instincts before that of the psychologists. The psychologists had never accepted McDougall's way of treating the instincts with anything like unanimity. Both Thorndike and Watson had criticized these broad instincts as poorly established, and had not seen much promise in the notion of native driving forces. The main question with the psychologists was as to how far complex behaviour patterns were inherited rather than built up by learning. Doubts began to be raised whether complex actions were ever provided by nature; it might be that only simple movements were provided by nature and all complex activities were learned. The conditioned reflex held a suggestion that such learning might go on unintentionally, as well as very early in childhood. The outcome of this discussion has been to make psychologists more critical of instincts than they were.

But this psychological revision of the doctrine of instincts has nothing necessarily to do with purposivism. You notice that there are two problems mixed together in this debate on instinct. The one is that of how far behaviour patterns are native and how far they have to be learned; and that is the question that has most interested psychologists and on which they have developed this critical attitude of wanting to be shown before they will admit that a behaviour pattern is native. The other problem is that of native impulses or primary motives. It would not seriously damage McDougall's system of psychology if he were forced to admit that almost all the behaviour patterns of fear, anger, love, curiosity, self-assertion, and the other instincts were acquired by learning and conditioning. What he requires of his instinct of combat or pugnacity is not any well-developed fighting performance, but the tendency to resist interference with angry energy. If man is so constituted that he does this, using whatever means he has at his disposal, then we may speak of a primary pugnacious motive which operates in many forms at various levels of behaviour.

To very many psychologists, however, the notion of primary motives as ' driving forces ' or ' primal sources of energy ' smacks of a sort of mythology that they hope to get away from. Instincts as entities remind them of the old ' faculties.' They doubt the existence of any such entities or separable factors. So the mass of psychologists, who may be called positivistic in their attitude, seem little impressed by the instincts as conceived by McDougall ; while those who hunger for entities are usually better pleased by Freud's dualism of two great instincts, or by Jung's monistic libido, than by McDougall's pluralistic list of instincts, closer to the facts of behaviour though the latter certainly is. To the existentialist, McDougall appears to be dealing with hypotheses rather than with direct data of experience, and he seems further to be so obsessed with the social uses of psychology that he scarcely tarries at all in the purely psychological field. The Gestalt psychologists seem to have no great objection to the instincts, and they have a definite place for goal-seeking in their system, where it appears in the guise of ' closing the gap ' and is related to physical dynamics. Upon the whole, purposivism, as represented by McDougall, occupies an uncertain position at present, and is probably not receiving the attention that it deserves.

THE PRESENT STATUS OF PURPOSIVISM

McDougall, however, expresses himself [1] as much encouraged by a recent drift of opinion in his direction. He says :

[1] In C. Murchison, editor, *Psychologies of 1930* (Clark University Press), p. 3.

Fifteen years ago American psychologists displayed almost without exception a complete blindness to the most peculiar, characteristic, and important feature of human and animal activity, namely, its goal-seeking. All bodily actions and all phases of experience were mechanical reactions to stimuli, and all learning was the modification of such reactions by the addition of one reaction to another according to the mechanical principles of association. . . . Now, happily, all is changed; the animal psychologists have begun to realize that any description of animal behaviour which ignores its goal-seeking nature is futile; . . . they are busy with the study of 'drives,' 'sets,' and 'incentives.' . . . Much the same state of affairs prevails in current American writings on human psychology. . . . Motivation, after being almost ignored, has become a problem of central interest. Yet . . . we are in a transition period; and all this recognition of the purposive nature of human activity is partial and grudging.

What he means by calling the present recognition of purposiveness ' partial and grudging ' is that most psychologists seem determined to reduce purpose to something simpler. Hunger, thirst, fatigue, drowsiness, and perhaps sex craving are said to be organic needs, 'tissue needs,' chemical conditions of the organism which predispose it to certain types of activity (or inactivity). Fear and anger are similarly related to the organic state produced by the sympathetic nerves and the secretion of the adrenal glands.[1] Thus several of the primary motives seem cared for by physiological conditions of the organism. Psychologists have had more difficulty in reducing to simpler terms the purposes or intentions which are so common in daily life and which have no obvious relation to these physiological conditions. In a simple instance, you need some object for a particular purpose, and go hunting for it. You persist in this activity for some minutes till you find what you want. This persistence probably does not point

[1] Compare E. J. Kempf, ' The Autonomic Functions and the Personality,' *Nervous and Mental Disease Monographs*, 1911, No. 28.

to any 'tissue need' similar to hunger or thirst; but psychologists have suggested that some sort of a set or adjustment of the brain or of the whole organism starts into activity when the goal-seeking starts and persists internally till the goal is reached. Vague suggestions of this sort have been made with the object of reducing purpose to something physiological, and with the object of enabling a stimulus-response psychology to take care of the fact of purpose without adding any new fundamental category to its system.

McDougall is not satisfied with any such 'partial and grudging' admission of purpose into psychology. He now defines his purposive psychology in clear and forcible terms: [1]

My task is the more difficult one of justifying the far more radically purposive psychology denoted by the adjective 'hormic,' a psychology . . . which asserts that active striving towards a goal is a fundamental category of psychology, and is a process of a type that cannot be mechanistically explained or resolved into mechanistic sequences.

Instead of starting with reflexes or elementary sensations, or anything ultra-simple, McDougall maintains that the proper line of attack in psychology is to proceed from the known to the unknown. What we know best, in the realm of behaviour, consists of clearly purposive actions. We should, then, use definitely purposive behaviour as the basis for our understanding of behaviour which we do not understand so well. The typical behaviour is purposive. Purpose is not exceptional and out of the ordinary run and to be explained by reducing it to something simpler. Purpose can properly be carried over into abnormal psychology, as has been done by the hormic psychopathologists, Freud especially; and purpose can properly

[1] *Psychologies of 1930*, p. 4.

be carried over into animal psychology and applied to all behaviour which, objectively considered, has the characteristics of goal-seeking. Speculatively, McDougall even conceives of hormic physics and chemistry, and of the possibility that the ultimate science may be teleological and not mechanistic.

We stand then, according to McDougall, at a parting of the ways in psychology. We have to answer the question whether human mental activity is mechanistic or teleological. We have to choose our answer and direct our psychology accordingly. I admit for myself that I am unable to see this question as a true dilemma. It appears to me that purpose and foresight are only possible when we have some knowledge of mechanistic cause and effect. Fully developed purposive activity requires the use of means to gain our ends ; and a means is a cause of which the end is the effect. We perform a certain act and await its consequences which are what we really intend. We throw a bucket of water on a fire to put it out, depending upon a known causal sequence. It further appears to me that anticipations and purposes arise as effects in the stream of natural processes and that they have their effects in that same stream. Some psychologists, after going to great pains to show that purposes, etc., are really natural and behaviour processes, yet are afraid to deny them any causal efficacy. Such hesitation is groundless, for if a purpose belongs in the world of natural processes as an effect, it belongs there also as a cause.

Nor do I see anything wrong with accepting purpose as a true fact and at the same time seeking to reduce it to physiological processes which taken singly are not purposive. It is just another case of the whole having properties that are not to be found in the parts. It is no more absurd than when, after throwing a ball, you turn to the physiologist and ask him to explain what muscles participated in the movement, though no one of those muscles can be said to have thrown the ball. Purpose, as we know it, inheres only in complex activities, and if we permit ourselves any dissection of these complex activities, we are bound to miss the purpose in our analysed product.

McDougall, like Jung, connects the hormic theory with the physicist's theory of energy. ' Hormic activity . . . seems to involve liberation of energy potential or latent in chemical form in the tissues. . . . But it refuses to go beyond the facts and to be bound by current hypotheses of physical science ; and it refuses to be blinded to the essential facts ' of goal-seeking. McDougall appears not, then, to postulate a special hormic energy different from the physical.

Purposive activity, as McDougall repeatedly insists, is known to us as mental activity, with perception of the situation, anticipation of the effects to be produced, striving toward the goal, and satisfaction when the goal is reached. These are the essential facts which hormic psychology refuses to slur over. It admits knowing as a genuine fact, yet does not fall into intellectualism, since its primal fact is the ' urge to live, to be active.' Admitting striving and satisfaction, it has a place in its system for values, and provides the factual basis for the philosophical treatment of ethics and aesthetics.

The great value of a purposivistic psychology, as McDougall sees it, is that it furnishes the fact of purpose for the consideration of philosophers who wish to understand the course of nature in its main outlines. Is the process of nature purely mechanistic, each new event being fully accounted for by what has occurred before, or is there any room for teleology in nature ? If psychology brings forward the fact of purpose as an ultimate fact, then philosophy has something to stand on in supporting teleology. Thus purposivism is in touch with the more philosophical physicists and biologists who are examining anew the relations between science and religion. Many scientific men seem to feel that the nineteenth century mechanistic philosophy of the universe, and especially of life, has broken down of its own weight. ' Emergent evolution ' is the most familiar symptom of this unrest. Without himself accepting emergent evolution or any other one of the new philosophies of nature, McDougall [1] insists with all force upon the psychological fact of purpose, and believes it sufficient to establish the reality of ' teleological causation,' a type of causation in which striving toward an anticipated goal has a real influence on the course of events. He proposes to recognize teleological causation not only in the field of human behaviour, but also, without question, in the field of animal behaviour. He strongly inclines to extend the concept to cover the growth of organisms as well as their behaviour ; and if it covers the development of the individual organism, why not also the evolution of all living creatures ?

Thus McDougall's purposivism goes far beyond the psychological field, and the psychologist is not in duty bound to take issue with it. One is free to accept it, to reject it, or to leave it aside, in its philosophical aspects, while still maintaining the psychologist's own proper freedom to deal fully and frankly with purpose and goal-seeking as he finds them in his own field. McDougall's purposivistic philosophy is as irrelevant in psychology as is the electron-proton philosophy of Weiss. Now that psychology, after a hard struggle, has achieved the right to be unphilosophical, we should use eternal vigilance to maintain our freedom. Any individual psychologist has, of course, his individual freedom to apply his psychology to philosophical problems. There is no reason why one of us, as well as one of our brothers in the other sciences,

[1] *Modern Materialism and Emergent Evolution* (Mehuen, 1929).

should not feel at liberty to take a flyer now and then in the speculative market, though one is pretty sure to find oneself in the position of a lamb. But we should keep our speculation apart from our regular business as psychologists, and certainly not make any claim on our fellow psychologists to join our outside ventures.

CHAPTER VII

THE MIDDLE OF THE ROAD

BESIDES the historical background which we have sketched in for each of the psychological schools in its turn, there is of course a general contemporary background consisting of the psychology of our time in the broadest sense, with all its variety of interests and all its manifold researches into both scientific and practical problems. Without some indication of this contemporary background, our picture would still lack perspective and might convey an exaggerated impression of the part played by the schools in the psychological activity of the times. In closing our survey, then, we may well leave the schools behind for a brief glance at the general body of contemporary psychologists.

Suppose we should organize a world's tournament or Olympic contest of psychologists, and should assemble the two or three thousand of them on some large field, with banners raised here and there as rallying points for the adherents of the several schools—a banner here for Freud, a banner there for Adler, one for Jung, one for McDougall, one for the Gestalt school, one for the behaviourists, and one for the existentialists, with perhaps two or three other banners waving for schools which I have not mentioned. After all the loyal adherents of each school had flocked to their respective banners, there would remain a large body in the middle of the field, or on the grand stand, ready to watch the jousting. How many would thus remain unattached ?   A majority ?   I am convinced it would be a large majority.

Nor would this unattached majority consist simply of the hoi polloi, the little fellows.   We must not imagine that we have had before us all the leaders in present-day psychology, even though we have seen many who are not adherents of any of the schools.   Certainly, the leaders of each of the schools are men of outstanding ability ;   but so are many other psychologists whose leadership is due to their output of important research rather than to any effort on their part to found systems in which the field of psychology shall be defined and its general aims and methods laid down.   Certain psychologists lead in the study of intelligence, others in the study of sense perception, others in educational or industrial or abnormal or animal or social psychology ;   but these leaders, while they have pupils and followers, have not generally founded schools of the sort we have been considering.

To name a selected few out of the many leaders who deserve mention—since clearly we can name but a few— might appear invidious except for the fact that we are merely sketching in a background, merely calling on a few who can worthily represent the great majority.   Instead, however, of calling on any of my American colleagues, I will present a bit of statistics in support of my statement that many leaders are to be found outside of the schools. Since the founding of the American Psychological Association in 1892, thirty-seven of its members have successively been elected President as a mark of honour and distinction. Of these thirty-seven, I have found occasion to mention fourteen, but only two of them as adherents of any of the schools.   Of the whole thirty-seven, about six might have been named as adherents of one or another school.   Thus a survey of the schools is a very different matter from a survey of the present state of psychology.

A Few Foreign Psychologists outside the Schools

In Great Britain, as compared with the United States or with Germany, the number of professional psychologists is small, but their standard is high. Professor Carl Spearman of the University of London (born 1863) might be cited as the head of a school, but it would be a different type of school from those we have described. Americans are familiar with the long-continued debate between him and Thorndike on the nature of intelligence, Thorndike supporting the view that intelligence is an aggregate of numerous special abilities that are unrelated to one another except as each depends on facility of learning, and Spearman, while recognizing a special ability for each type of performance, insisting also on a general ability which enters in some degree into every variety of intelligent bahaviour. This general factor he designates as 'g,' and the debate over g has gone on actively for twenty-five years. Spearman has recently reached the conclusion that this general factor consists very largely in the ability to see and use relationships. Though both Spearman and Thorndike have had many pupils and fellow-workers, I do not include them among the schools, because the issue between them is in a fair way to be settled by evidence. Their controversy, then, is one of the standard scientific type, rather than a debate between rival schools. The issue between two such schools as the behaviouristic and existential cannot be settled by evidence but is a matter rather of preference.

Another British leader of wide influence is Dr. C. S. Myers of London (born 1873), who holds a special place in British psychology as the first director of a psychological laboratory in the kingdom, that at Cambridge, and who more recently has become the director of the National Institute of Industrial Psychology, a unique institution in the applied field with much important research work already standing to its credit.

Passing now to Germany, we think first of the three great original leaders of experimental psychology, already mentioned : Wundt, Stumpf, and G. E. Müller. Each of these men used both introspective and objective methods. None of them can be reckoned with the existential school, which did not take definite shape till after their own lines of thought were well established. Each of these men has had many pupils, who have not, however, remained a compact body or school. Wundt's pupils, for example, include men of such diverse tendencies as Titchener, Cattell, and Spearman. Wundt's successor as head of the Leipzig laboratory is his pupil, Felix Krueger (born 1874), a student of phonetics and of folk psychology. He has developed a ' totality psychology ' not identical by any means with the Gestalt psychology. For one thing, Krueger points out that the configuration perceived at any moment is itself imbedded in a total feeling. Feeling to him is a more basal fact than figure and ground.

Several active members of the Gestalt school are old pupils of Stumpf, and it is interesting to notice the master's comment on their enterprise.[1]   He speaks of :

Gestalt, upon which certain young scientists of my acquaintance, who have done commendable work in studying its laws, would like to base, it seems, not only the whole of psychology but even logic itself. . . .

I have never endeavoured to found a school in a strict sense ; and have found it almost pleasanter, certainly more interesting, to have my students reach different conclusions than to have them merely corroborate my theorems.

---

[1] In C. Murchison, editor, *A History of Psychology in Autobiography* (Clark University Press, 1930), vol. i. pp. 433, 441.

Professor E. Spranger of the University of Berlin (born 1882) is a prominent representative of what is called the 'understanding psychology' in distinction from explanatory or causal psychology. To 'understand' is to grasp the meaning of something. The meaning of anything comes from its contribution to the value of a larger whole, as the meaning of a word in a sentence arises from its helping to carry out the intention of the speaker. To understand an individual, we have not to dissect him nor even to consider him as a whole apart from his environment, but to see him in his social relationships and to see his present in relation to his past.

Of Müller's pupils, there are two whose work is somewhat akin to that of the Gestalt school, but who are definitely not adherents of that school. E. R. Jaensch (born 1883), now professor at Marburg, has laboured unremittingly on the problems of visual perception, and of late years has awakened special interest by his studies of the life-like mental images, called 'eidetic' images, evidenced by many children. David Katz (born 1884), professor at Rostock, besides his work on child and animal psychology, is noteworthy for his demonstration of the curious ways in which colour perception is affected by the conditions in which the colour is seen.

Of the numerous other active German psychologists of the day, William Stern (born 1871), a pupil of Ebbinghaus, is notable for the many lines in which he has been a pioneer. He was a pioneer in Germany in the study of individual differences, in the introduction and development of intelligence tests, in the study of children and youth, and in the field of applied psychology. He started the work on the psychology of testimony. Much in the manner of McDougall, he has used his psychology as a stepping-stone to a philosophy which he calls personalism. A person, he says, shows unity in multiplicity and thus reconciles in himself the categories of existence and of value.

Eminent psychologists, not attached to the schools, are to be found in several other countries. In Switzerland we find Professor E. Claparède of Geneva (born 1873), who has developed, independently of Dewey and Angell, a functional psychology much like theirs and with similar applications to education. He founded the Institute Rousseau for the study of children, a very active centre of such study. In regard to associationism, he makes the pregnant remark that association itself does not account for the control of association that is so much in evidence in such intellectual activities as reading and adding. The control, he says, must lie with the factor of interest. His conception of sleep is important ; he finds it cannot be explained as a mere poisoning by fatigue products ; it must be a positive response of the organism, and practically an instinct. A peace-loving man and the Permanent Secretary of the International Congress of Psychology, Claparède believes that the debates between the schools represent wasted energy which might go into more productive channels.

Italy has many active psychologists, none of whom, as far as I know, are definite adherents of the schools, though Vittorio Benussi (1878–1927), late professor at the University of Padua, was a member of the Austrian Gestalt school that started with Ehrenfels and his study of Gestalt quality. Benussi made important contributions to the study of form perception, and also is of interest as the inventor of the breathing test for the detection of lying.

S. de Sanctis (born 1863), professor of psychiatry and of experimental psychology at Rome, has many claims on the psychologist's attention. Besides much varied work on the neuroses and psychoses, he was an active pre-Freudian student of dreams in normal and abnormal subjects. Probably his chief field has been child psychology, including the study of abnormal and subnormal children. He devised one of the earlier and simpler test scales for indicating degrees of mental deficiency.

Professor F. Kiesow of Turin (born 1858) was an early pupil of Wundt and studied also with the Italian physiologist Mosso, well known to psychologists for his ergograph and his studies of fatigue in human muscles. Being well disposed toward the young science of experimental psychology, Mosso in 1895 set aside a portion of his own laboratory for it and secured Kiesow to work there. Kiesow presided over this embryo psychological laboratory for ten years, and then was given a more adequate laboratory of his own, in which he has had many pupils and has concerned himself particularly with sensations of taste, touch, and bodily position, and also with feelings and images. In his theoretical views he adheres closely to Wundt, and with regard to the Gestalt psychology, while recognizing that it has undertaken a very important line of study, contends that it has by no means done away with the fact of elementary sensations or with the need for continuing their study.

In France, also, there are many active psychologists, none of whom belongs definitely to the schools, except that there may be some psycho-analysts among them. The French remain strongly attached to the association psychology, but recognize the need of combining with it something of the hormic principle. Their own philosophers, as Paulhan and Bergson, have anticipated much of the fundamental teaching both of the hormic and of the Gestalt psychology. The French psychologists are inclined to maintain an open-eyed independence and eclecticism.

Binet's successor in the laboratory at the Sorbonne is Henri Piéron (born 1881), whose work in the main has been not along Binet's line of intelligence testing but in experimental and physiological psychology, animal psychology, and the study of brain injuries during the war. Piéron might easily be counted as a behaviourist, since he was led by his animal studies to define psychology as the study of behaviour before Watson used that formula. But Piéron is perhaps clearer-headed than the American behaviourists. He sees no difficulty in including in behaviour study the study of sensations and even of images, and no necessity for calling into question the individual's testimony to his own consciousness. Only, in order to become available as scientific data, introspections and impressions must somehow be registered in objective and socially intelligible form, as in words. All such registered experience is objective behaviour, and therefore all psychologists really employ behaviour data. The only question is as to the degree of intelligibility and reliability possessed by a given type of data ; and there is no sharp line to be drawn in this respect between the objective and the subjective methods in psychology.

Another prominent French psychologist, Georges Dumas (born 1866), professor in the University of Paris, and concerned in his own researches very largely with the emotions, is further noteworthy as the leader of a large group who are collaborating in the comprehensive *Nouveau Traité de Psychologie*, the first volume of which appeared in 1930. The point of view of this group is that introspection, in spite of its difficulties, has proved itself fruitful up to a certain point, and is really indispensable in psychology, since it has certainly furnished the suggestion even for the objective studies that have been carried on, and also supplies the personal interest which one finds in psychological results. French psychology is strong for the biological basis and also for the social setting of the individual's activities. Furthermore, in accordance with its long tradition, from the days of Charcot and earlier, it leans heavily on psychopathology. The dynamic principles

15

of Freud appear to the French as less of a revolution from those of Janet than we have been accustomed to think.

Finally, though we could easily find eminent representatives of psychology in many other countries, we may bring this hasty survey to a close by taking note of the official psychology of Soviet Russia, which endeavours to base itself upon the philosophy of Karl Marx, the philosophy known as ' dialectic materialism.' The effort is in part to illuminate the known facts of psychology by aligning them with this philosophy, and in part to use the philosophy as a guide toward new research and discovery. The Marxian type of materialism has a place for consciousness as a real fact, a new quality, emerging when the physical processes reach a certain degree of complication. Hence, these Russian psychologists reject both the exclusively subjective and the exclusively objective types of psychology. Introspection is not to be rejected, but its findings always need confirmation by objective methods, since the latter approach more closely to the fundamental physical processes. The individual, they go on to say, must be studied from the social as well as from the biological side, since he is a product of his social environment. He is a product of his economic class and of the work which he is called on to perform in the world. So the individual should be studied as a member of an economic or vocational class, and the study of class psychology is fundamental as well as practical. K. N. Kornilov (born 1879), director of the Institute of Experimental Psychology in the Moscow State University, is one of the leaders of the Russian group.

THE TREND OF PSYCHOLOGY

These few names that I have cited are intended to give you an impression of the great middle body of psychologists who do not admit allegiance to any of the schools, though some incline more toward one and some more toward another. They refuse to swallow the medicine offered by any one of the schools. They refuse, that is, to adopt the system or theory of any of the schools. Such refusal need not in the least debar us, if we belong in the middle group, from recognizing good work wherever we find it. If the existentialist presents a good analysis of heat sensations, or of colour experiences, we accept it with thanks. If the behaviourist shows by experiments on little children how conditioned fears may arise, we are free to use that finding in our own psychology. If the Gestalt psychologist should show that all learning depended on some degree of insight, we should revise our conceptions of learning accordingly. If the purposivist convinces us that the individual is never passive when a stimulus reaches him, that is another important point to be dealt with. If the psycho-analyst opens our eyes to the importance of sex motivation, we thank him for that. Every genuine positive result is meat for the psychologist who is not prejudiced by loyalty to a particular brand of psychology. Not taking his start from a preconceived system, but rather working his way toward a system by fitting together the facts as they are discovered, the unattached psychologist may be derided as a mere eclectic ; but that need not disturb him, for certainly any system that is put forward to-day must be revised as research sheds new light on our problems. There is much unexplored country in front of the psychological advance. Each school, glimpsing from some vantage point a little of the lay of the land ahead, prepares an outline map of what we may expect to find, and offers it as a guide for our explorations. But these outline maps differ one from another, and cannot all be right. The probability is that no one of them is entirely right and that many surprises are in store for the psychological explorer.

I would not leave the impression that this great body of

unattached psychologists is in perfect harmony on all matters of psychology. If we divided our whole body of psychologists into groups according to their preferred fields of research, such as animal psychology, child psychology, abnormal psychology, test psychology and individual differences, educational psychology, social psychology, industrial psychology, the psychology of sensation, of perception, of learning, of emotion, and so on, we should soon find controversy going on in each of these special groups. We should find debates on the nature of intelligence, on instinct, on learning, on heredity versus environment, on race differences, on motivation, on the unconscious, as well as on many topics of narrower scope. We find similar controversies in any science, controversies due in part to the human nature of the scientists, and in part to the inconclusiveness of present evidence on the questions in dispute.

But while controversies and debated questions are frequent in all the sciences, schools such as we have been considering seem almost peculiar to psychology. It may be there are some in the social sciences, but at least in the natural sciences at the present time they are hard to find. From time to time you have men appearing with new and startling theories, like Mendel's theory of heredity or Einstein's general relativity, and controversy immediately breaks out over such theories, some authorities tending to accept and others to reject them. But Einstein, for example, has not exactly founded a school. What he did was to deduce consequences of his theory which could be checked up by observation. Physicists and astronomers, being in a position to make the necessary observations, put the deductions to the test. Some of those who thus tested the theory probably hoped they would verify it and others that they could give it a knock-out blow, but they all agreed that evidence was what was required.

As the evidence obtained favoured the theory, the general attitude toward it quickly became favourable, though there are still physicists who are opposed to it, and who hold that the evidence is insufficient to warrant even a tentative acceptance of the theory. But in all this there is little resemblance to our psychological schools and their debates.

Sometimes we middle-of-the-roaders worry a little over the existence of schools in our science. They look like an indication that all is not well and that psychology does not yet know where it stands or what it has to do. But every one must admit that the activity of the human individual is extremely complex. The schools may take their origin from just this complexity. Many sides of the complex activity offer themselves for study, and a psychologist who becomes absorbed in one side is sure to stress its importance and may come to regard it as the ultimate thing. The existentialist becomes interested in sensation and regards that as ultimate ; the Gestalt psychologist becomes interested in perception and regards the patterning which he finds there as the ultimate fact of psychology ; the behaviourist becomes interested in motor and glandular behaviour and takes that as ultimate ; the purposivist regards purpose as ultimate ; and so it is with Freud and the libido, with Adler and the will for power. All the schools are emphasizing something that demands emphasis, and serve a useful function in the progress of psychology. We evidently should define our science broadly enough to cover the positive findings and emphases of all the schools.

So if you ask me which school to choose for your own, I should be inclined to advise you to stay in the middle of the road. We must remember that the middle-of-the-road group are not simply the left-overs or those who cannot make up their minds. Sometimes, with a slight change in the figure of speech, we middle-of-the-roaders are said to be sitting on the fence, and to have, in bad individual cases, an inveterate tendency to sit on the fence. Well, in support of this position it may be said that it is cooler up here and one has a better view of all that is going on. But I like the middle-of-the-road figure better, because it brings out the continuity of this group. They were there in 1900, before the schools appeared, and have been progressing steadily since, and have achieved a considerable increase of knowledge in the course of thirty years. So I see no reason to urge my younger confrères toward this or that school. But if any one needs the excitement, or needs the stimulus of a special loyalty, then I advise him to choose by all means for himself.

The schools are certainly not without value. Each emphasizes something worth while. And each, because of the resistance it encounters from the general body of psychologists, is stimulated to great activity in the effort to show the value of its own line of study. No one can fail to see that the great research activity of the Gestalt school has been motivated largely by their desire to make out a good case for their general theory. In the same way, Watson's fine enterprise in studying the emotions of babies and their conditioning was motivated by the desire to demonstrate the value of his chosen line of attack.

One reason why psychology has not split up during the past two decades into several separate groups is the need of each school to present its case before the general body in the hope of winning support. Another reason is found in the large body of those who remain in the middle of the road. And a third reason is that, after all, all psychologists are cultivating the same general field, the activities of the individual, human or animal, child or adult, normal or abnormal. For these and perhaps yet other reasons, the psychologists of the world have shown much more solidarity than one outside the group might expect from the loud noise of conflict that has reached his ears. It is true that some of the more intense members of the different schools have cared little for general meetings of psychologists ; and it is true that the medical psychologists have mostly flocked by themselves, being occupied with their practical problems and with their own debates. Yet, on the whole, one can say that psychologists get together very well. At one of their meetings or congresses you will find much fraternizing and much mutual respect between members of the different groups. You will see the lion and the lamb lying down together so comfortably that you cannot tell which is lion and which lamb.

If you ask me which school is going to prove its case and win out—so forcing me against my will into the dangerous rôle of a prophet—I shall answer, all and none. None—for the contentions of each school seem to me not of the nature of hypotheses that are susceptible to proof or disproof by the weight of evidence. Each school represents certain preferences for one or another type of study and dislike for certain other types of study. Since each school is likely to prove its case to this extent, that its chosen line of study will be recognized as fruitful, it follows that none can be dislodged and consequently none can win the field entirely for itself.

If you ask me how long the schools of to-day will endure, I can only answer that each still shows plenty of youthful vigour. Each has some distance to go to explore the part of the field that it has specially chosen for its own. More-over, so long as more extreme variations of the theory of each school remain possible, so long we can anticipate that young radicals will continue to push the theory toward its extreme. At the same time, largely through the influence of the middle-of-the-road group, the wearing down process already begun is sure to continue. Material from this side and from that is bound to find its way into the middle and become the general property. The harmonizing process is at work and the central science of psychology will take over whatever it can, while the schools keep up their supply of one-sided pronouncements.

I do not wish to imply that compromise and the golden mean between any two extremes represent the sure guides to the views that will eventually prevail. It may even happen that views that now seem altogether extreme will prove their merit. But I am reasonably sure they will never crowd out other views that now appear incompatible, when these views are such as our schools chiefly profess. What I mean is that hypotheses suggested by one or another school and seemingly bound up with the major tenets of that school will be found not to be so bound up but to hold without regard to their relation to the slogans of the schools. I can imagine, for instance, that goal-seeking, insight, and the conditioned reflex may all be found to be indispensable in the process of learning.

You must have enjoyed the bold beauty of such a valley as Chamonix or Yosemite, and when you learn their story you see that their peculiar charm comes from their being young valleys in a geological sense. They have been carved out by glaciers which have only recently retreated and left behind these bold cliffs and outbursting waterfalls. Erosion has not gone far with these valleys, but by degrees it will wear down the cliffs to gentle slopes and convert the waterfalls into mere mountain streams. What a pity !—but the glaciers may come again.

Our beautiful psychology may owe its peculiar type of exciting charm to the fact that it, too, is young. The glaciers of philosophy—of course, it must be philosophy—having but recently retreated to the high mountains, have left us our cliffs and waterfalls. But erosion has already set in and is labouring to reduce the boldness of those cliffs and the exciting dash of those waterfalls. Even where El Capitan now rears his massive front we may expect in time to see but a gentle wooded slope. What a pity!—but the glaciers may come again. Meanwhile, the older, well-cultivated valley certainly has some advantages.

APPENDIX

SUGGESTED READINGS

WITHOUT aiming at bibliographical completeness, the following list of readily accessible books may serve as an introduction to the active supporters of the several schools. The questions appended to some of the references suggest the topics treated in outstanding passages.

I. General Readings

C. Murchison, editor. *Psychologies of 1930.* Clark University Press, 1930. This collection contains articles by representatives of each of the 'schools' and by other psychologists of the present day.

G. Murphy. *An Historical Introduction to Modern Psychology.* Routledge, 1929. All the schools are presented, with their historical background.

E. G. Boring. *A History of Experimental Psychology.* The Century Co., 1929. This work is very full on existential psychology and its antecedents, and contains brief accounts of behaviourism and the Gestalt psychology.

C. Murchison, editor. *A History of Psychology in Autobiography.* Clark University Press, 1930. Vol. i. These autobiographies are interesting both from the personal side and because of their brief and frank presentation of their author's views. The present volume contains the autobiographies of several psychologists mentioned in the text, of Janet, of McDougall, and of Stumpf, Claparède, Kiesow, Spearman, and Stern, as well as those of several others who have not been mentioned, though prominent in the history of our time.

E. B. Titchener. *Systematic Psychology : Prolegomena*. Macmillan, 1930. A critical discussion of other conceptions of psychology, leading to the formulation of the existentialistic position.

H. P. Weld. *Psychology as Science*. Methuen, 1928. Existential psychology and its relations to animal, social, and abnormal psychology, etc.

J. B. Watson. *Behaviour : An Introduction to Comparative Psychology*. Henry Holt & Co., 1914. Chapter I is the original pronouncement of the behaviouristic position.

J. B. Watson. *Psychology from the Standpoint of a Behaviourist*. 3rd edition, Routledge, 1929. The author's most complete statement of his psychology.

J. B. Watson. *Behaviourism*. Routledge, 1930. A popular treatment.

W. S. Hunter. *Human Behaviour*. University of Chicago Press, 1928. Pages 1–16 contain a general statement of the author's view.

W. Köhler. *Gestalt Psychology*. Boni & Liveright, 1929.

W. Healy, A. F. Bronner, and A. M. Bowers. *The Structure and Meaning of Psycho-analysis*. A. A. Knopf, 1930. This book assembles systematically the statements of Freud and his pupils regarding the various conceptions of psychoanalysis.

II. Selected Passages, with a Question on Each

E. B. Titchener. *A Beginner's Psychology*. Macmillan, 1918, pp. 1–36. In what ways must psychology, to be scientific, be different from common sense ?

I. P. Pavlov. *Conditioned Reflexes*. Oxford University Press, 1927, pp. 1–32. What is Pavlov's conception of a conditioned reflex and of the way in which it is established ?

J. B. Watson. *Behaviourism*. Routledge, 1930, pp. 1–47. Has Watson justified his position in eliminating the older concepts of psychology—consciousness, sensation, perception, will, etc. ?

A. P. Weiss. *A Theoretical Basis of Human Behaviour*. R. G. Adams & Co., 1925, pp. 3–26. What relationship does Weiss emphasize between stimulus-response and what he terms the cosmic movement continuum ?

K. S. Lashley. *Brain Mechanisms and Intelligence*. University of Chicago Press, 1929, pp. 157–74. In what respects does Lashley's theory go counter to current reflex theory ?

Bertrand Russell. *Philosophy*. Allen & Unwin, 1927, pp. 123–36, 161–75. What difficulty lurks in the behaviourist view that ' objective observation ' is a perfectly straight-forward reading of facts ?

C. K. Ogden. *The Meaning of Psychology*. Harper & Bros., 1926, pp. 93–131. How the insight theory of animal learning differs from the trial and error theory.

C. K. Ogden. The same, pp. 161–202. Ogden's conclusion on the controversy between introspectionism and behaviourism.

W. Köhler. *The Mentality of Apes*. Harcourt Bruce & Co., 1925, pp. 1–25, 235–45, 275–77. What is 'insight' from the Gestalt point of view ?

K. Koffka. *The Growth of the Mind*. Routledge, 1925, pp. 125–50. How the infant's mental activity begins and develops, and how it is tied up with his motor activity.

A. Alpert. *The Solving of Problem-Situations by Pre-school Children*. Teachers College, Columbia University, 1928, pp. 1–27, 36–45. What types of behaviour are taken to indicate ' insight ' in young children ?

R. H. Wheeler. *The Science of Psychology*. T. Y. Crowell Co., 1929, pp. 16–25, 75–85, 502–3. In what way does the configurationist claim to bring psychology into line with science in general, and to do so better than any other school ?

R. H. Wheeler. The same, pp. 11–16, 137–55, 197–200. What introspection accomplishes, and how its result are related to Gestalt psychology.

R. H. Wheeler. The same, pp. 470–500. The Gestalt critique of the view that behaviour consists of a combination of reflexes.

S. Freud. *General Introduction to Psycho-analysis*. Allen & Unwin, 1920, Part III. How would you state the difference between Freud and Pavlov with respect to their method-ological approach ? What is the rôle of fear in mental life, according to Freud ?

A. Adler. *The Neurotic Constitution*. Routledge, 1917, Intro-duction and pp. 1–123. How do the terms, ' will to power' and ' will to seem ' find application in Adler's system ?

A. Adler. The same, Introduction, and pp. 1-123. *In-*

dividual Psychology. Routledge, 1924, pp. 23-31, 317-26. Difference between Freud and Adler in the rôle assigned to sex.

C. G. Jung. *The Psychology of the Unconscious.* Routledge, 1916, pp. 8-41, 139-56. According to Jung, what is the function of undirected thought ?

W. McDougall. *Outline of Abnormal Psychology.* Methuen, pp. 1-73. How are McDougall's criteria of behaviour purposivistic ? Why does McDougall wish to replace the tropistic theory by the hormic theory ?

W. McDougall. *Outline of Abnormal Psychology.* Methuen, 1926, pp. 1-29. How do psycho-analytic concepts lead to McDougall's views ?

W. McDougall. The same, pp. 518-40. How does McDougall describe the formation of character ?

L. L. Thurstone. *The Nature of Intelligence.* Routledge, 1924, pp. 1-56. What is Thurstone's main objection to the stimulus-response formula ?

W. H. R. Rivers. *Instinct and the Unconscious.* Cambridge University Press, 1922, 2nd edition, pp. 34-70. How does Rivers's conception of instinct aline him with one or another of the schools ?

W. Brown. *Mind and Personality.* University of London Press, 1926, pp. 17-47. How does Brown's attitude toward vitalism aline him with regard to the schools ?

INDEX

239

PRINTED BY
MORRISON AND GIBB LTD.
LONDON AND EDINBURGH

Drever: Psy. of Educ.

Living organism is

1. System of forces or activities
   nor a complex structure

2. self-maintaining

3. self-determining

Psy. the science wh. studies human
behaviour, interpreted in mental
terms.

Dif. from ani. psy. wh. is pure
behaviourism — part of biological science—
That human being has exper. or conse.

Also diff. from older psy. in that it
sought to throw light on destiny of
human soul, instead of applying results
practically.